UNRAVELLED

UNRAVELLED

THE INSPIRATIONAL TRUE STORY OF
A JOURNEY OUT OF DARKNESS

VIKIE SHANKS, LYNNE BARRETT-LEE

THISTLE
PUBLISHING

First published in 2014 by:

Thistle Publishing
36 Great Smith Street
London
SW1P 3BU

ISBN 13: 978-1-910198-45-2

www.thistlepublishing.co.uk

Dedication and Acknowledgements

This book is dedicated to all of the people who have played such a vital role in enabling us to survive over the past few years, without whom we would certainly not be where we are now. I may not have expressed my thanks adequately but you are all constantly in my thoughts and my gratitude will be everlasting.

Also to all of the loyal and enduring friends I have made over many years who, I know, are always there for me through thick and thin. My life is by far the richer for knowing you all, including all of the young people I have met through the children, all kind hearted, fun and willing to help. May our friendships long endure.

And, of course, to my seven incredible children - without them I would be lost. My love, respect and admiration for all of you is beyond words. My only wish in life is that we stay as close and strong as we are for all eternity.

To Andrew, my agent, without whom this book would never even have been started, never mind come to fruition. His stalwart support and dedication to seeing this book through to publication has been constant. He believed in me long before I believed in myself.

And last, but by no means least, Lynne Barrett-Lee, my ghost writer who has given me more than just a book. Our journey together writing this has been one of intense discovery for me, and with her amazing insight I now understand myself better than ever before. She is a true friend and I can never thank her enough.

Thank you to all the people that have touched our lives. You are all precious gems that I treasure in my heart for all time.

Vikie Shanks
June 2014

CHAPTER ONE

MISSING

15th September 2007

The 15th of September. Something was supposed to be happening today, wasn't it? It was an important date: I'd known that for months. I must have, because it was fixed so firmly in my head. But not in my diary. Which was odd, because my diary was my lifeline. Life was complex, and just lately had become even more so. So much so that I knew nothing would get done unless I remembered to make a note of it in my diary. What with the ailing business, our huge family home almost sold – *finally* – and the complicated lives of seven children to organise... And yet there'd been nothing about this date. It was really strange.

It was, however, the most beautiful morning. Dry and sunny, it was the sort of early autumn day that stopped you from mourning the end of summer - the light bright and coppery, the sky blue, the air warm; a time when the woods and fields that surrounded our house seemed to be limbering up in readiness for their annual display of colour. And it would be some display, too - a riot of red, orange, ochre and an intense canary yellow, before the big leaf-fall that would transform the whole landscape.

Twenty-one long years. It felt impossible that we had now had our last summer living here, and I could hardly bear the thought of moving out. But move out we must. We had no choice: we had seven children to think about. And as I gazed out of my bedroom window, listening to the sound of them playing downstairs, I mentally steeled myself. It was happening. It *had* to happen. I threw on a thin summer dress and went downstairs.

Our dining room was as sparse as the rest of the house, my husband Paul, over the years, having systematically removed everything he deemed unessential to our lives. Every ornament, painting, knick-knack and item of soft furnishing was now gone – he'd even removed most of the furniture. We had been minimalist long before minimalist became fashionable. Sparse before sparse was considered chic. I was used to it now, even though I hated it. The magnolia walls and complete absence of anything personal meant it felt like we lived in an institution rather than a home. Which, on one level, we did; it had become normal over the years to come down and, with Paul having decided to make changes overnight, not even know which of the rooms in our necessarily huge, rambling home would be the dining room that day. But to go against what Paul wanted could be little short of dangerous. So we put up with it. What else was there to do?

The children were already gathered at the dining table, eating breakfast. Because it was a Saturday, they were allowed to have chocolate-coated cereal, and I could see my son, Osborn, seated in his special electric chair, scoffing his bowlful down appreciatively. Pippa, the youngest, and the other of my children to have cerebral palsy, was in the chair her physiotherapist had supplied for her. The rest were doing what they usually did variously reading, sitting quietly, squabbling or chatting – to them, it seemed, this was just another day. I sat down with them, still feeling this sense of unease about it, even so. What *was* it that was bugging me? I wished I knew.

'Is something supposed to be happening today?' I asked them. I was met with blank faces.

'Happening?' asked Jamie. Jamie was my eldest. Now sixteen, she had grown into a very pretty young lady, with the same long brown hair as had all of her sisters, and the kind of assertive personality common in a first-born.

'Yes,' I said. 'I just have this sense that something's supposed to be happening today, but I can't think what it is. I thought one of you might know.'

'I felt that too,' Lorie piped up immediately. Together with her twin sister, Mirie, Lorie was now twelve, and perhaps the most like me of all of my children. She'd always had a keen perceptiveness about her, so I wasn't surprised she shared my nagging sense that there was something important I'd forgotten. 'I don't know what it is, though,' she added, shrugging.

Jamie frowned and shook her head, as if to speak for the rest of them, as she often did. 'Mum, you're *both* imagining it,' she said firmly.

'Oh well,' I said, deciding to push the feeling from my mind. Perhaps she was right. Perhaps I *was* imagining it. I was tired, after all; Paul and I had worked the evening before, running a fun casino for a conference over in Stratford while Jamie had babysat her younger siblings. It was only around 15 miles away, but it had been late by the time we'd put away all the fiddly bits, loaded the van and driven home. If whatever it was turned out to be important, I'd know soon enough. Besides, the weekly Tesco shop was calling so what I really needed to do was run back up to my bedroom, grab some shoes and get on with it.

It was just as I stood to go upstairs that my mobile phone rang. It was a client waiting for Paul to deliver some games. That was our core business; we supplied games for events; and not just the games, either. We would provide the whole package. About half of our events took the form of casinos, for which, as well as full size games and tables (designed and built by Paul) we'd create the whole look, involving plants, atmospheric lighting and so on. Our other speciality was providing giant indoor 'fun' games. We had giant Jenga, giant Connect Four, giant Tiddlywinks, and so on, as well as a range of table football, air hockey and arcade games. The latter 'hi-tech' stuff was supplied by a long-standing business associate, Geoff, who as well as being a colleague was a very good friend. We did anything from weddings to conferences, and every-thing in between, though most of our work came from businesses. We'd been doing it for twenty years now – far too long for me. I was no longer enjoying it – had I ever? – And now we were separating, I was anxious to become more financially independent, so that I wasn't reliant on a shared endeavour.

I felt my heart sink when I realised who it was. I'd screwed up big time on this one. This guy had been in touch weeks ago to hire a couple of our giant games for his event, and had arranged to collect them the previous evening. I'd completely forgotten about it for some reason. It was such a small part of our business that something bigger must have pushed it from my mind, which was all over the place lately anyway, what with everything else that was going on. Feeling guilty about it – it was obviously my fault, after all – I'd told Paul I'd be happy to drive the ten miles or so to where all the games were currently in storage. But he'd said no. *He* would do it. He was adamant. And when Paul made his mind up, that was the end of it. I knew better than to argue the point, even though I still felt pretty guilty that he had to pick up the pieces from my error. To go against Paul was to incite a row, and the aftermath of a row was weeks of stony silence – all of which had a terrible effect on the children, so it was never worth it. Little did I know he had his own reasons for not wanting me there.

But here we were, Saturday morning, and the client still didn't have his equipment.

'I was just wondering when they'd get here,' he said. 'Your husband told me he'd deliver them first thing this morning, and it's now almost eleven. Is he on his way?'

Given our late night, I naturally assumed Paul had simply overslept. Though I wouldn't know, because he no longer slept in the house with us. As we were separating everything was in flux; we were going through the process of completely changing our plans for the future, and Paul had already hired a solicitor to commence proceedings for divorce. I'd only wanted us to separate for 6 months initially, to take stock, see if we *had* a future as a family - the result of an epiphany I'd had almost 3 years before. I'd been standing in a pound shop – I can recall the details vividly - when, while looking at biscuits, I had this sudden and intense realisation that contrary to the premise I'd been living my life by, I did not have to be tied to Paul for life. One thing was certain - I was no longer prepared for either myself or the children to be subjected to what was beginning to feel like his almost psychopathic behaviour. We could, and perhaps should, live apart from him.

Since then we'd been sleeping separately; me in the house with the children, and him – having just unilaterally decided he was doing it (and I didn't argue) - in the mobile home we had in the garden. It was sited around a hundred yards from the house, near the derelict stable block, and had originally belonged to my father. It was a caravan my father had bought years back, the plan being that it would be somewhere he could stay if the time ever came when he needed to live close by in order that we could care for him. I'd been reluctant to agree to such a thing, as there was little love lost between us by that time. But Paul had been keen and, since we'd inherited it, it had indeed become a useful extra room for when anyone came, and a place he could send the kids to, to watch videos, when they were 'under his feet' - sometimes for hours at a time. Until he moved in there himself three years ago, anyway.

I apologised to the client and told him I'd sort everything out, then turned to Jamie, who, like the rest of the children - bar Kacie, who was still in bed - had now finished her breakfast and was sitting chatting and laughing. It was always this way; despite their various problems the children were always such a happy little bunch when it was just us. Put Paul into the mix and the atmosphere changed. Suddenly you could cut the tension with a knife.

'Jamie, do me a favour,' I said, as I got up to go and finish dressing. 'Can you nip up to the Atlas and wake up Daddy, please?'

How I wish I had gone myself that day. I should have; knowing there was a client involved – a potentially cross client, too. So there was bound to be some sort of confrontation with Paul and I had no business putting it on my daughter. She agreed to go, though, but not before going upstairs to fetch Kacie, and not before Kacie had eaten some breakfast herself – which obviously delayed things significantly.

I was up in my bedroom getting my shoes out when my mobile rang again. It was Jamie and I was cross that she was being so lazy; ringing me when she could just as easily have walked back to the house to speak to me - something she did often, and which always drove me mad. But the way she said 'mum', with such a terrible tremor in her voice made me forget all thoughts of anything but what she'd say next.

'What?' I said. 'What, Jamie? What's the matter?'

'Mum,' she said quietly, 'if ever there was something really urgent, this is it.'

I ran down the stairs not knowing what to expect. Paul was so volatile and so dramatic that it could have been anything or nothing – probably nothing, I thought, as I emerged into the garden, but seeing the girls running towards me brought me up short.

'Go inside,' Jamie said to Kacie, just as they reached me. She didn't argue. And it was only once she'd gone that I noticed that Jamie had something clutched in her hand. 'I wanted to try to spare Kacie this,' she explained, her voice wavering. She then thrust several pieces of paper towards me, and as I took it I could see how much her hand was shaking too. I took the pages from her and immediately saw what appeared to be a title; Paul had written '*This is my suicide note*'.

But that was all I read, because at that exact moment I heard the distant chime of the doorbell. It made us both start, and with Jamie beside me, I rushed there with a sense of foreboding. I wasn't expecting anyone and something told me it would be related to the sheaf of paper I now held in my hand. But the children beat me to it. It was Jamie who opened the door, to find a policeman and policewoman, both of whom stood on the doorstep with expressions that told me in no uncertain terms that they weren't popping in for a coffee.

'Are you the wife of Paul Shanks?' the policewoman asked me. I could see the concern in her expression.

I was in a daze by now. Everything was happening too fast for me to keep up.

'Yes,' I said.

'And do you know where he is?'

I told her I didn't. She looked anxious. 'Then can I have a word with you, please?'

I stepped out of the front door and onto the driveway, trying to manoeuvre them as far away from the younger children as possible. The policewoman waited till we were out of earshot before explaining the reason for their visit. 'We've received a call from your husband,' she said quietly, 'telling us he was about to kill himself, and asking us to come round, take away his body and take care of the children.'

'Dad's car's down at the bottom of the field, Mum,' Jamie said, 'Next to the woods.'

My mind raced. At the bottom of the field? Down by the woods? Why would he park there? He never parked his car there. My car was invariably parked on the front drive, but since he'd been sleeping in the caravan Paul would always park his car by the back door, or, if not, up by the caravan itself.

'What did he sound like when he called you?' I asked, trying to make sense of what was happening. I couldn't get my head round the idea of Paul calmly calling a police station and informing them he was about to take his own life. Yet according to the policewoman, he had been exactly that – calm. And apparently methodical, too. 'My daughters have found this,' I said, remembering what I still held in my hand. I lifted the note Jamie had given me, and the policewoman almost snatched it out of my hand.

It was at that point, I think, when I began to feel stirrings of real unease. Perhaps something bad had indeed happened. Even so, the greater part of me felt it wouldn't be *that* bad. Paul was an attention-seeker, and this drama was very much in character. Perhaps when they found him – and I was sure they would soon find him – it would be to find that he'd just taken a few pills.

Jamie pointed the way and the police immediately set off at a run, heading round the side of the house, in the direction she had pointed, down the field towards the woods where his car was parked. They shouted behind them that we should all remain in the house, but I ignored them. I was still barefoot but I ran after them anyway, telling Jamie to stay in the house and look after the younger ones.

By the time I reached the car the police officers had already run past it and into the woods, obviously having established that Paul wasn't inside. Even from a distance, I could see that there was so much blood on and around the car that it was clear he had made a serious attempt on his life. The policewoman saw it too. As I watched, she looked ahead, into the thicket of branches her colleague had plunged into, then very deliberately put the note down by the car, presumably to collect later. I felt my heart begin to thump – the sight of the blood was just so shocking – but found the presence of mind, once she'd gone, perhaps not realising I was still behind her, to lean down and snatch it up from the grass.

At that point I stopped, and considered it properly. I'd not had a second to do so, but now that I did, I knew it was all horribly real. The 'note' was actually two notes, each stapled separately, one of which seemed to have been written a few weeks ago – and in third person, oddly – and the other, the writing style markedly different, much more recently. I didn't stop to read more than was needed to get the gist of it; that everything that had led to this was my fault. The police were right. I shouldn't follow them on into the woods. I should do as they told me and get back to the children. They would be distressed and confused and would need me. They loved their father – despite everything he'd done, they still loved him, because that's how children are programmed to feel. Despite being terrified of him, and the fact that he barely registered their existence (except when they annoyed him) they loved him. Pippa and Osborn would be okay – they were too young for what was happening to properly sink in yet - but the older five would, I knew, need me there.

Clutching the note, I ran back up to the house to see them clamouring at one of the windows. It was a room that was currently empty, following one of Paul's remodeling projects, and they'd obviously gathered there as being the best place to see.

'It's okay,' I said when I got to them and we all trooped into the sitting room. 'The police are here now. They'll find out what's going on. Try not to worry.'

Jamie and Kacie, however, didn't look like they believed me. And with good reason. Only now did they have a moment to tell me exactly what they'd found when they'd gone down there. The company van was parked up by the Atlas at that time, and the door to it was hanging wide open. And Paul's current diary – his precious diary, which he NEVER left unattended – was lying on the seat just inside, with his glasses.

Baffled, they'd made their way back to the house, only to see his car parked at the bottom of the field. They could see him sitting in it and thought that perhaps he'd decided to have a cigarette. He'd been behaving oddly in previous months; for so long a non-smoking teetotal vegetarian, he'd been drinking heavily, eating meat again, and smoking. He'd been trying to keep the smoking secret, so, with Jamie not wanting to 'catch' him red-handed (we all knew anyway) she decided to leave him to it for a few minutes before going down.

When they emerged from the house the second time, however, it was to find that Paul had disappeared. And when they went down to the car Jamie discovered two crucial things; the suicide notes on the seat, which were blood-spotted, and more blood on the ground by the driver's door. Thank goodness she had the presence of mind to protect her younger sister from the trauma of that particularly gruesome sight.

God only knows why but I then looked at the wedge of paper in my hand, and immediately saw what I should do. I needed to make a copy. I needed to be able to read and digest the contents, and whatever happened – whether Paul was still alive or already dead – I knew the police would take it away. And I needed to know. I felt strangely clear-sighted about it. I needed to know by what process Paul could possibly have decided that him deciding to do what he'd done was down to me. Yes, I was human and fallible and had made mistakes along the way, but Paul controlled our lives, *all* of them, in every way possible, and all I'd ever done – in the face of increasingly bizarre and cruel behaviour – was try to keep him happy. I took the letter to the photocopier on my desk near the dining room and started photocopying all 14 pages.

In the time it had taken me to copy the note in its entirety, the whole property had been overrun by police. Cars and vans of all shapes and sizes seemed to have arrived from every direction; numerous police cars, an ambulance, a CCTV van, a fire engine… there must have been something like a dozen or more vehicles in attendance, and something approaching thirty personnel. I had even heard the familiar thud-thud-thud of an approaching helicopter. I'd looked out of the window as I'd done the copying, and had seen the word 'Police' on it. And as it circled over the fields and woods, presumably searching for Paul, another one had joined it – this time what looked like the Air Ambulance.

The two helicopters continued to circle each other for what seemed like an eternity, but were probably about twenty minutes. What were they doing? I wondered, neck craning to watch them as the copier spewed paper. What could they see that I couldn't? What was Paul playing at? Another police van arrived then, this time carrying a tracker dog and handler, and they also headed off down to the woods. It was becoming unreal; beginning to feel like some-thing out of a TV drama. There were so many police by now, most in the woods, presumably still searching, but three or four on the patio, helping to distract the children. Pippa was only six and she was trying on a hi viz jacket, laughing as it trailed along the ground as she walked, genuinely enjoying the moment, too young to have a sense of the enormity of what was happening. What *was* happening? Where the hell was Paul?

It must have been nearly midday when we watched the Air Ambulance helicopter finally land, Osborn whooping with excitement when he saw it touchdown in the field, while the police helicopter peeled off and flew away again. I watched the rotors slow and saw what looked like a doctor jump down and run into the woods. A police officer sprinted up to the house shortly after and told us that the tracker dog had found Paul and that he was conscious and talking. This lightened the mood considerably; we were all just so relieved he was still alive.

'There,' I said to the children. 'The doctor's with Daddy now. He'll be okay.' I said it several times. 'It's okay. He'll be okay.' Though, privately, I wasn't yet so sure. I had no idea what Paul had done to himself, but as the minutes ticked by and no one had returned to reassure us, I thought of the children, the mess we were in, the terrifying future stretching ahead of us, and felt this panicky rush of questions rising up in me. What would happen now? Would he finally be seen by a doctor who could assess his mental health? What would be the repercussions regarding the ongoing sale of the house? How would the business continue to run? Did this mean he'd at last get the help he needed? *Why* had he done it? What were his parents going to say? Had he done it to try and stop the move - to keep us together? My mind was all over the place.

Another twenty minutes or so passed before anyone emerged from the woods, and as soon as I saw them, I feared the worst. He might have been conscious before, but their body language, even at some distance, told me he was conscious no longer. It was the doctor and the Critical Incident Officer who were walking up the field towards me, and as I watched them, I could see from their expressions what they would tell me. In that instant I knew Paul was dead.

My mind snapped into gear then. I couldn't let them reach the children before they told me, so I ran down to meet them and head them off.

'He's dead, isn't he?' I asked the men as soon as I reached them.

'Yes' the doctor said. 'I'm sorry. There was nothing we could do.'

I just stared at him, my whole world evaporating into this black hole of hopelessness. Had there ever been *anything* that could have been done about Paul? I didn't think so. He had been beyond help for so long now. And he had always been capable of anything.

No, this was it. I was on my own now. And I was terrified.

Chapter Two

HANGING ON THE TELEPHONE

London, Autumn 1983

It was a weekday when the phone rang. And it was early. Much too early. Not because I had any sort of aversion to early mornings. It was just that today was a rare day for me. No early modelling shoot to go to. No casting to turn up for. So the thought of the resultant lie-in had been precious indeed.

I opened one eye. The bedside clock told me it was just past 6am. I groaned and rolled over. It surely couldn't be for me, could it? So I rolled over, pulling the duvet over my head. If I ignored it, it might go away.

But it refused to be ignored. It just continued to ring and ring. And back in those days there was no handy plummy voiced BT lady who'd tell the persistent caller to go away. Ring ring, ring ring, ring ring... It carried on incessantly. At what point, I wondered irritably, would the caller give up? Ten minutes? An hour? A day?

I yanked the covers off. *Someone* had to answer the wretched thing, and it looked like that someone had to be me.

'Hello!' said a woman's voice, when I finally dragged myself into the hall to answer it. She sounded bright and wide-awake, and also oblivious to the fact that I could cheerfully have strangled her right then. 'Is Paul there?' she chirruped gaily. 'This is his alarm call!'

Paul? Who was Paul? I had never heard of anyone called Paul. Well, not in the sense that I *knew* anyone called Paul. I was at home in my flat, and my flatmate was called Rob. Why would someone be asking for a Paul? But they were. 'I'm his mother,' the lady explained, in response to my half-asleep enquiry. 'He told me to call him on this number…'

It finally clicked. Whoever this Paul was, he was obviously staying here overnight. I just hadn't been made aware of it. Which was nothing unusual. My flatmate was also my landlord and he was always having friends over; you couldn't move for bodies on the living room floor some mornings. Something which, had I been more properly awake, I might have twigged.

But this was different anyway. What sort of overnight guest would have already organised an alarm call? And from his mum, no less. What was he? *Twelve*? I told the lady on the phone that I'd go and see if there was anyone called Paul currently in residence and sure enough, one look in the living room confirmed it; there was certainly someone in there who might answer to that name. No, not a spotty adolescent in need of a nudge to get up for school, but a fully grown bedraggled male, who, once he'd pulled himself upright – he'd obviously been in an even deeper sleep than I had – turned out to be quite tall and seriously good looking.

And definitely too old to be getting phone calls from his mummy.

'If you're Paul, there's someone on the phone for you,' I told him, making my irritation plain. I raised my eyebrows. 'Your mother, apparently.'

And with that, I turned around and went straight back to bed. I didn't register any more than that, because I wasn't interested in doing so. I wasn't seeing men. Wasn't seeing them as in going out with them, and wasn't really noticing them, period. I'd just escaped from a horrible, violent, controlling relationship. I'd had it with men. No matter how good they looked on rising. I was fast asleep again in a matter of moments.

It would be two months before I next saw the man who was to become my husband, and in the interim, I didn't give him a second thought. My life was full and busy and, for the first time in a long time, I was happy. I was twenty five – still very young - and most importantly I was free and single. And I had no wish to return to the constraints of any kind of relationship, because the one I'd recently escaped from had required exactly that – that I physically escape from him while he was away.

His name was John, and he was seventeen years older than me, but most importantly, he was both violent and extremely jealous. Once I'd left him, I vowed that that was it. I had just the one plan; to become independent. To work hard at my modelling career, which was just taking off for me, and to save enough to put down the deposit on a London flat of my own. Oh, and keep men at arm's length for a while.

And where Paul was concerned, I was clearly doing well. He didn't appear at the flat for a couple of months after that – not while I was there anyway - so the next time I saw him it was a moment before I recognised him. It was a Saturday morning and I was sitting in the living room chatting to my friend Alison. Back in those days, phones came in only one variety - the fixed to the wall kind. And the phone socket being nowhere near the sofa where I was curled up, I'd stretched the wire half way across the room and plonked the phone on the coffee table, the remaining distance being covered by the receiver cord. So perhaps it wasn't one hundred percent Paul's fault that when he came in to get something, he tripped over the wire, and sent the phone itself crashing on to the floor.

Nevertheless, to my mind, he should have seen it anyway, so as he arrested his own headlong fall into the fireplace, I gave him a withering look. 'Some *idiot* has just dragged the phone to the floor,' I told Alison, provoking a red-faced and very hasty exit.

Paul seemed to be a regular visitor after that, and I avoided him as much as I could. Not to be rude, but just because our first two meetings had been such negative encounters that I just wasn't impressed with my first impressions. He was also a rather irritating presence. When he was there, he and Rob would invariably commandeer the kitchen, sitting together, looking earnest, writing what sounded like rather mediocre songs – and basically getting under my feet. It was a constant reminder of what I most wanted at that point. To get out of flat-sharing and have a place of my own.

But it seemed I wasn't going to be able to avoid Paul forever. He was obviously an old friend of Rob's and, from what I could see, a good one, and it was therefore understandable that our paths kept on crossing. And a couple of weeks later, they finally converged. I'd had my older brother Philip down from Coventry for the weekend, and on the Saturday evening, having been out all day visiting the military museums he was keen to visit (he was keen on military history to the point of obsession), we returned to the flat to find Rob had some mates round - Paul included - and they invited us to come along to the local pub with them.

My brother didn't drink (he was also a devout 7th Day Adventist), so the idea didn't really appeal to him. I quite fancied going out, however, so we did. Looking back, it was one of those decisions that I could equally have made differently. And how differently might my life have panned out then? As it was, Paul and I got talking in the pub that evening and, to use an expression that's probably only so clichéd because it's true, once we started we didn't want to stop.

It would be easy to say that I was attracted to how he looked, and there was no doubt that Paul's striking resemblance to David Cassidy might have been a factor. There was also the glamour factor – he was a singer-songwriter, trying to carve out a career in music, and though he seemed very driven, there was something self-effacing about him; he certainly seemed to have realistic ambitions.

And, by the sound of it, he had reason to be optimistic, too. Though he was only getting the odd bit of work currently, as an extra for film and TV, he was hoping to secure a third season with the Black and White Minstrels tour as a singer/dancer in the chorus, as he'd done for the two previous years. He'd already had West End theatre parts in *Jesus Christ Superstar* and *They're Playing Our Song* as well, so his hope of one day getting a record deal or clinching a starring role didn't seem unreasonable.

But much as these details impressed me, it was his mind that most entranced me - that, and how in tune we seemed to be intellectually. Whatever the reason, we spent almost the whole evening talking only to one another, and when we returned to the flat we ended up in bed.

I left the flat early the following morning, along with my brother, leaving Paul still asleep in my tiny single bed. Though it had not been quite the night of passion to end all nights of passion (Paul had a slight deformity in his penis which he would go on to explain could make love-making challenging), I was still intrigued by the person I'd spoken to at such length the night before.

But I had to go. My brother and I were off to visit our maternal grandfather, who I'd only tracked down a year previously. He'd never been a part of our lives, and finally getting to meet him was part of the reason my brother had come down to stay. I was keen to meet him too, partly because I'd lost my mother when in my teens and had so many questions, so there was no question of re-arranging it.

But there was no doubt that there was something else on my mind as we chatted to his second wife and some of their children that were visiting; would Paul still be at the flat when I returned?

How had that happened? I wondered, as I said my fare-wells to my brother and rushed back to Belsize Park that afternoon. I didn't know, but it was clear that something had happened between us as when I opened the living room door to find Paul sitting on the sofa, playing his guitar, and felt an unexpected rush of pleasure that he'd hung around.

He was in the middle of writing a song – which sounded like it was shaping up to be quite a good one - and I didn't want to disturb him. He just looked so engrossed, so com-pletely focused on what he was doing; playing a few chords, trying some lyrics with them, stopping, making adjust-ments, scribbling notes on his A4 pad, then going through the sequence again. So I just sat and watched him, marveling at a kind of creativity I'd never seen in action before, know-ing that I really wanted to get to know him better.

Chapter Three
SHIFTING SANDS

My childhood had not been a happy one. Every family has its ups and downs, its peculiarities, its idiosyncrasies, but ours was a family that was perhaps always going to flounder, because it was built on what turned out to be such shifting sands.

My mother's own childhood had been far from idyllic. Born to young parents at a time when marriage was considered a lifetime commitment, whatever the circumstances, she and her brother had their lives turned upside down very young. She was just eleven when my grandfather moved a second woman in, Gertie, with whom - after he expelled my grandmother from the marital bed - he went on to have a further five children.

My grandmother apparently made the best of it, but it must have been an intolerable situation for them all. No wonder, perhaps, that my uncle joined the RAF at 16 and left, or that my mother fell pregnant at 17. Fortunately my grandmother supported her – and at a time when pregnancy outside of marriage was considered almost criminal - and my eldest brother Philip was born.

Phillip was three when my mother met my father. He was a Sergeant in the Motor Transport Department in the

RAF, and, unusually for the times, and no doubt to my grandmother's relief, married my mother despite her illegitimate son.

My mother's life as a military wife began almost immediately, when my father was posted overseas, firstly to Germany. She hated it. She felt as though she was always having to 'keep up with the Joneses' and struggled socially - something I now realise is probably due to the fact that she was almost certainly on the autism spectrum. And as my father was always on the entertainment committee and very often in charge of the entertainment for whichever base they were on, life involved accompanying him to events and meeting lots of new people, which must have been extremely difficult for her.

But there were clearly difficulties within the marriage, too. Another son came along when Phillip was eight, who they called Tony (he is also autistic), and when he was three, he fell out of a bedroom window and badly broke his leg. This prompted my mother – inconsolable, and convinced it was God's revenge on her – to confess that Tony wasn't my father's child, either. He was the son of a half Maltese man she had met when they were stationed in Malta.

The marriage continued, however, and by the time I was born, they were stationed in Aden, now the South Yemen. I would know nothing of the circumstances of my brother's parentage till much, much later, but for my father this was to be a watershed moment – at last he would have a child who was biologically related to him. But, to his evident dismay – and he was never less than vocal about his feelings about how little he felt women were good for - I was born the wrong gender.

Understandably, given that my mother had failed to provide him with his own son, ours was never a happy or harmonious home. The military lifestyle is a challenging one for a child at the best of times – it was always hard to try and make friends and settle into an environment only to have to leave and become the outsider again somewhere new. But far worse was that home – which should, above all, be a place of constancy and safety – was a place of discord at best and violent rows at worst.

It was also a place of anxiety and fear. When I was six my mother suffered a breakdown and was bedridden for weeks. It therefore fell to my eldest brother Philip, now in his mid teens, to take on the lion's share of looking after Tony and I. And he seemed to have his own ideas about what 'looking after' me might involve; it was a period that marked the start of what turned out to be regular episodes of sexual abuse. It was never full-on rape but even at my young age I knew his hands and fingers shouldn't be doing what they were doing, that my own hands definitely shouldn't be caressing him in the places he made me caress, and that the way he was kissing me was wrong. Fortunately, when I was eight, he joined the army, so was away a lot, but his inappropriate behaviour towards me continued intermittently until I was about 12 when I suddenly found a voice that said 'no'.

But if Philip's behaviour towards me caused me confusion and anxiety, it was my parents' behaviour towards one another that caused me fear. I was frightened all the time, and spent a lot of time hiding under my bed to escape the ferocity of their fighting, even though it wasn't directed at me.

School, by contrast, provided a less volatile environment; one in which I thrived academically. I was a bright, inquisitive child, always wanting to know everything about everything, and, being also hard-working once my mind was occupied with facts rather than fear, was soon moved up several classes above my age-group.

Sadly, this made it very difficult for me socially. Surrounded by older children who didn't see why this little kid should be put in *their* class, I was a perpetual outsider, branded 'weird' from the word go. My friendship group therefore comprised every other 'weird' kid in the school: the little disabled kid, the kid who smelled because her rather odd family kept donkeys... Bullied mercilessly, in the days before bullying was robustly dealt with, we could only cling together and make the best of it.

But it was a promising start that was not to be fulfilled. Aged 11, and having done extremely well in my 11+, I was awarded a scholarship to Perse private girls' school in Cambridge, close to where my father was then stationed. I didn't want to go – struggling socially myself, given my peripatetic childhood, I was too concerned that the local girls would brand me a snob, and my parents, no doubt because of the financial implications, didn't try to talk me into it, either. So instead I went to the local high school, an academic hothouse intent on grooming girls for Oxbridge.

All the good work of my primary years soon unravelled. Though my IQ was very high, my interest in academic studying was now very low, and I came to hate the endless essay writing and swotting. Soon I was floundering at the bottom rather than cresting the wave and by the time I was 13 I was offered a choice: either going down a year or transferring to the local comprehensive; a cruel irony, given that doing the opposite had so blighted my primary years. I chose the latter, hoping for a less competitive, and hopefully more creative environment, but, as the new girl from the 'posh' school, I failed to thrive there either. Friendless and disorientated, I was systematically bullied for the next three years.

But there was a much more defining moment soon to come. It was shortly before my 16th birthday when my mother developed a dry, persistent cough, which no one initially thought very much of, but which within two weeks saw her admitted to hospital, extremely ill. No one knew what was wrong, but tests seemed to point towards her kidneys, and as I was apparently a match I spent the period immediately before my birthday gearing up to donate her one of mine. Events soon overtook this, however. She fell into a coma, and I remember the nurse sitting us down and telling us that there was very little possibility that she'd survive.

It was the sort of news that is almost impossible to take in. How could it have happened? How could she have been fit and well one minute, and on a life-support machine the next? And there was no time to gather thoughts and try to hope for the best, either. She died seven days later of a cerebral haemorrhage. She was just 47, literally, the day before she died. And because my father fell apart and was unable to handle it, I spent my own birthday organising her funeral.

The pain of losing my mother was visceral. She had never been a 'cuddly' mother, probably due to her autistic brain; indeed, I think she struggled to have a close relationship with anyone. And on an emotional level, she often felt 'not quite present'. Perhaps as a result of the stress of her fractured marriage she'd had a breakdown when I was small, and was permanently a bit spaced out on anti-depressants and sedatives from then on. But on a practical level she had always been brilliant. So though I never felt quite loved I had always felt cared for, and losing my anchor so young left me feeling frightened and alone.

But it was a revelation about my father, just days before we were to bury my mother, that was to prove the most pivotal in my young life. As was the norm in my family, it began with a row, one I was having with my father about Phillip. He felt his eldest son hadn't done as much as he should have to help with the funeral arrangements and I disagreed. Phillip was married by now, and though he didn't have children (he'd decided against doing so, as he'd been diagnosed with a form of muscular dystrophy) he had his work and his wife to think of, and, as I pointed out, he *had* spent the last four days staying with us.

Such a silly thing, but one that triggered such a big thing; my father telling me, in his fury, that he'd never liked Phillip much anyway, as he wasn't his son – he told me he'd been the result of an affair my mother had had as well. This was obviously an untruth in itself, as I would find out a bit later (Phillip's birth pre-dated him), but hard on its heels came the next revelation – that Tony wasn't his biological child either. There was only me – I was the only one of his three apparent offspring to actually carry his genes.

Reeling from shock now, as well as grief, I went straight to my grandmother's flat and asked her to verify the story. Here I heard the real facts about Phillip and Tony and also something that would send my whole world out of kilter – that I almost certainly wasn't my father's biological child either.

My father never knew this – nor would he ever, I decided; not from me – but my mother had apparently taken her own mother into her confidence about this many years previously, and a check of the dates soon confirmed it. Unbeknown to my father, I was the child of a Flight Sergeant my mum had met in 1957, when he was away, having been posted to Aden.

It was a great deal to take in, and affected me deeply, colouring almost every aspect of my life. It was also heightened and intensified by other knowledge that I gained shortly before my mother's death. I'd been diagnosed with polycystic ovaries when I was 15 and a half, following concern over my extremely erratic periods. At the time, I hadn't cared. I'd already decided I didn't want children, so it mattered little. But now, even though I hadn't changed my mind about becoming a mother, I had this strange sense of dislocation: genetically, I had a cloudy past and no future either. My mother was dead, my brothers were only my half brothers, and my father – the man who'd bullied and beaten my mother, the man who'd caused me so much pain throughout my childhood, the man who I currently lived with and who'd go on to put me through so much more - wasn't actually my father at all.

I couldn't change the past, and the future was already set. I felt on my own, and would rather *be* on my own. I couldn't get away from my father quickly enough.

For all its traumas, my nomadic and emotionally challenging childhood had at least given me one thing; the precious gift of independence. Having been blessed with another gift – the relentlessly optimistic, 'glass half full' personality that had got me through so much - I got away from my abusive father when I was not quite 18. And though we continued to maintain a relationship (as I did with my brothers, even though Tony's autism made any kind of closeness difficult) I was determined that the man who helped raise me would no longer have a chance to bully me, shout at me, hit me or hurt me, so I was living independently very young, and finding my way - even training as a croupier and going out to Spain to live and work for a time.

The scars of childhood trauma manifest themselves long after childhood however, so although, by the time I met Paul, I'd got my life together in both practical and career terms, emotionally, I was still in a difficult place – I must have been, looking back; why else did I persist in falling for such unsuitable men? Men who tried to treat me in the same way my father had treated me? Wasn't that that last thing I needed in my life? Or was I just pre-programmed to seek out men who sought to dominate me and run my life for me because, in a skewed way, being controlled felt like the sort of security and stability that I had never known as a child?

A psychologist, as they say, would have a field day. But I knew nothing about psychology (not back then) and all I knew when I met Paul was that he seemed different from any man I'd met before.

Not that our early weeks were without trauma themselves. At the time our relationship 'proper' began, Paul was seeing another girl casually. And continued to do so a couple of times since we'd got together, too, which was something that, when I found out, naturally made me see red. Here I was, out of the frying pan of being with a man who was insanely jealous, jumping into the fire of one who apparently had no compunction about having two girls on the go at once!

It perhaps should have been my first indication that the man I was to go on to marry had such a massive problem with being honest where doing so involved letting the other person down. He didn't finish with her simply because he couldn't bear to have to tell her – complex psychological territory in itself – and only did so when I got so mad at him that dealing with my anger was a scarier prospect than breaking the bad news.

But once that was dealt with, we soon put it behind us, and, being besotted very quickly and very completely with one another, our romance began to blossom very quickly. Too quickly, perhaps, to allow rational thought to intrude, because, soon after, there was another sign that Paul had problems of that nature, that, again, I completely failed to spot.

At the time we met, I was working pretty consistently, having returned from my spell in Spain, modelling anything from tights and jewellery to clothes and shoes, as well

31

as lots of hair modelling as well. I also did a lot of show work, including London Fashion Week. I was what was known as a 'good working model' (a little like my trusty car) - shorthand for saying that though I would never hit the dizzy heights of supermodel, I would always be able to make a good living.

Paul, on the other hand was living much more precariously. Though he began staying with me at the flat most of the time, he was officially still living with his parents, working in a pub in East Sheen to bring in what money he could, while writing his songs and trying to get work in the entertainment business.

My car was therefore a bit of a lifeline for both of us and, as he didn't have his own – he'd written it off some months earlier - it made sense to put him on my insurance so that he could use it when I didn't need it. Which was fine till, one day, a few months later, when he went out for a drink with a friend in it and was breathalysed. He was found to be over the legal limit and duly convicted, getting a hefty fine (which I paid for him, as he had so little money) and being banned from driving for a year. But, though he was a fully-grown man of 28, he was absolutely adamant his parents must never know.

'But that's ridiculous!' I said, when he told me this. 'How can you hide something like that from them?'

'It's hardly going to be difficult,' he said. 'It's your car, so when we go round there you drive.'

I hated lies and secrets. I'd had enough of both to last a lifetime. 'But it's bound to crop up *sometime*,' I reasoned. 'Or I'll blurt it out by accident or something.'

'You must *not* blurt it out,' he said firmly. 'They *mustn't* know.'

It was a line he stuck to, despite any amount of consternation on my part. He was a grown man. And I did find it odd that he was so adamant that we keep it from them. It was hardly as if they were going to stop his pocket money, after all.

But I played along – after all, we were living some distance away, and there was no real imperative for him to tell them. Perhaps he just didn't want them to be disappointed in him, I reasoned. And if that were so, then so be it, even if it did seem a little silly. But how could I begin to fathom the complex, corrosive relationship they had with him? Particularly his mother. I hardly knew them, after all.

Chapter Four
ALL OR NOTHING

In the spring of 1984 Paul got a letter he'd been hoping for; the offer of another season as a backing singer/dancer for the Black And White Minstrels Show tour. A spin off from the iconic television series of the same name, it was a variety show that was at that time touring all the Butlins holiday camps around Britain. The TV show itself had long been off the air following accusations of racism (white singers were blacked up to look like traditional American minstrels) but the touring show was still a big draw, and, for Paul, it at last meant a regular paycheck for doing what he loved to do – singing and dancing - rather than working behind a bar.

It would also mean he'd be on the road from April to October. This didn't worry me unduly though, because by this time, my working life had changed as well. I was still doing a little modelling, but had been offered the chance to do something a little more exciting, working with a guy called Roger, who'd become a friend back when I was working and living in Spain. Roger had now set up a company which put on casino events for corporate clients. It was a completely new concept and his business had taken off very quickly, and he asked me if I'd be interested in coming along to some events and doing some dealing for him too.

Very quickly, I got more and more involved. I knew the boxer John Conteh quite well at the time, through my previous relationship with John, and he came along to an event with me, which pleased Roger no end, because that obviously made the night an even bigger draw. And as the weeks went on, I also became involved more in the running of the business; taking bookings, dealing with administration and – the part I loved best - loading the company van with the casino equipment and driving all over the country, setting up and running events myself.

I was in my element at work now – even though it had been an unlikely career change – and I was also in my element with Paul. Yes, we'd been parted, but I could drive and I was perfectly content to do so; happily heading off at any opportunity to whichever Butlins camp the tour was at, and staying in whichever Butlins chalet he'd been billeted in.

I must have driven many thousands of miles that summer, and as the weeks passed, I realised I was on another journey, too – one of complete infatuation.

It had to be that, in hindsight, because another side to Paul was beginning to emerge now, and it was increasingly clear that I had only two ways of being when I was with him. I was either deliriously happy, or at the receiving end of a horrible, violent fury that I seemed to be able to provoke for the most ridiculous of reasons and, having done so, was always at a loss to know how to stop.

The first of these happened quite early in the tour, when one afternoon – probably over-tired from the lengthy drive – I accidentally called him John, the name of my ex.

We were in his chalet, and had just finished making love. To this day I don't know how or why it happened, but it did. And it was like a nuclear bomb going off.

'How can you *possibly* love me?' he raged, 'if you can call me by *his* name?'

To which I had no answer, except to reassure him that I did - that it had simply slipped out, that I was obviously fatigued, that it had meant nothing at all. We'd only been discussing whether we'd drive back to London or not, after that evening's show. Nothing emotive. It had been nothing more than a random slip of the tongue.

'It's just force of habit,' I kept trying to tell him. 'I'm with *you* now, not him. And you *know* how I feel about him. He gave me *hell*, Paul – I've told you often enough!'

'But he *must* have been on your mind!' he yelled. 'Or why else would you say his name? If you loved me, you'd *never* say it by mistake!'

'Paul, this is ridiculous!' I shouted back. 'You're being completely paranoid – and for no good reason! God - how many times am I going to have to *say* that?'

The intensity of Paul's fury was terrifying to witness, but was nothing compared to what he did next. Presumably stung by my retort, he found a strength I never knew he possessed – sufficient to actually pick up the double bed we'd just been in, and hurl it across the room at me. Luckily I was able to dodge out of the way in time but the bed was not so lucky; a heavy wooden-framed affair, it hit the wall and immediately smashed into several pieces. And that wasn't sufficient to stop him either. He yelled at me for a further hour, saying the same thing over and over again, before storming out of the chalet and not returning. The next time I saw him, he was on stage doing the evening show.

Paul was made to reimburse Butlins £50 for the broken bed and was obviously contrite, but it was a watershed moment in our relationship. It marked the point when I could have walked away, having witnessed what I'd wit-nessed, but instead I made a conscious choice to try and put it into context and simply learn how to manage his emotions better. I'd be a steadying hand – I had a lifetime of experience, after all.

So I rationalised, anyway. And, as the memory of Paul's rage faded, so did my memory of the fear he'd invoked; it wasn't as if he'd hit *me*, after all – just taken his anger out on some furniture. And he hadn't *really* thrown the bed at me. He'd just thrown it. And, to be fair to him, I decided, my calling him by the name of my ex must have been hurtful. No, I hadn't done it intentionally, but with hindsight I *could* see it from his point of view.

And besides, all couples rowed from time to time, didn't they? And new relationships always required a degree of compromise and positioning. A relationship without con-flict was an odd one indeed, wasn't it? Not unless one of the parties to it was a doormat. And I was never going to be that. I had grown up in a house that was often seething with hurt and discord, listened to my father bullying my mother ceaselessly, and her just meekly accepting it. No, rowing with Paul wasn't nice, but perhaps it was necessary to stand my ground, particularly at this early stage, so that both of us knew where we stood with one another, the better to argue less in the future.

The trouble was that was that the arguments didn't get any better. The slightest thing could set Paul off on a rant about something and I would find myself dodging whatever he'd just thrown (and, yes, at me), while desperately trying to think of what I might have said or done that could have triggered his temper without me realising. But there was no pattern – it could be something as benign as my ironing a shirt he didn't ask to be ironed, or a random compliment paid to someone's performance, which he'd read as being a criticism of his own. He would read slights into comments where none were intended; he was clearly sensitive beyond a level I'd ever experienced before.

But as is so often the way, when it was good between us, it was brilliant. For all that I was fearful of Paul's quick and violent temper, I was every bit as much in love with his many positive traits. His sense of right and wrong; a moral code which chimed so well with my own. His sense of fun. His intellect. His tenderness. So it wasn't difficult to find myself accepting his shortcomings too – he had to accept mine, after all, didn't he?

By the end of the tour season, I had realised one thing. That Paul was possessive; one of those men for whom it was all or nothing. You were either with him or you were against him; no grey areas at any time. Which meant he found it almost impossible to accept that I had lived a life before him. The past – my past, particularly with John or anyone else – didn't, and mustn't exist. He couldn't bear it.

He was different from my previous boyfriend, though. Where John had been physically controlling, stopping me from going out with friends using threats or physically harming me, Paul never once tried to tell me what I could and couldn't do. He was more emotionally manipulative, turning things around so I felt guilty. Which, of course, I did. Because I loved him and wanted to make him happy.

When the Butlins tour ended, Paul moved back in with his parents. And it was at this point that it sank home to me that he had never really left. He was 28, but I was beginning to get a sense of his vulnerability; because he'd striven for so long to try and carve out the career he so wanted, he'd never really made the emotional break from his mother and father that he perhaps would have done if he'd got himself a nine-to-five job, and some early financial independence. As it was, he'd been beholden to them, because of living so precariously, chasing short-term contracts and casual jobs, so that he was free to write his music and go to endless auditions.

But perhaps he'd never felt the need to leave in any case. It was clear his parents cherished him, and that their approval of him mattered – and perhaps no wonder; he'd had such a very different childhood from my own. And there was no sense of him trying to break his mother's apron strings, either. Which was fine – how I'd longed to feel such security and love – but at the same time it made me pause for thought when he returned from the final tour dates, and announced that he had come up with a plan.

'You should move in here too,' he told me, and kept telling me over and over – a gentle but steady pressure that began on his return and which I initially dismissed as being a ridiculous notion – move in with someone's mum and dad at *my* age? Two months on, however, and I was beginning to see that not only was it something he wouldn't drop, but that, on a practical level, did have some merit. 'Of course it does,' he said one afternoon in my flat, just before Christmas. 'It's ridiculous you keep spending money on rent. And if we're there, we can be together so much more of the time then, too.'

There was some logic in this. It was some distance from the flat in Belsize Park to where his parents lived, and, as he didn't have a driving licence currently, I was the one forever shuttling back and forth. It was also true that I would be able to save up to buy somewhere of my own (our own?) so much quicker.

There was also the reality that despite the times when he frightened me, Paul by now had some sort of hold over me. Was it his sweetness? His undeniable charisma? His ability to constantly surprise and challenge me? Was it the knowledge that he was all but obsessed with me? Was that what I'd lacked – that real deep sense of being unconditionally loved? It was certainly beguiling to be so much at the centre of his universe. 'I've never met anyone like you,' he would tell me constantly. 'Never met anyone who understands me and supports me the way you do.'

And I was duly beguiled. I must have been. I had so many misgivings, but I managed to silence every one of them, including an important difference in our individual future plans. Paul wanted children; he said so all the time. But I couldn't have any - and neither did I want to. 'We'll just adopt,' he always said, as if he wasn't really hearing me; as if my stance was just temporary and would change over time.

I even silenced my concerns about his constantly doting parents (particularly his mother), and how, despite always seeking their approval, he sometimes seemed to treat like dirt – more like an ungrateful, ranting fifteen year old than a grown man. I silenced them by rationalising that this must just be how a proper family *was*; the intensely loving, nurturing kind that I had never had myself.

Yes, the doubts were still there - but who doesn't have doubts about relationships? How can anyone really know someone is 'the one'? Perhaps others might, but the scars of my childhood ran deep. I had no truly positive relationship model to draw on in the first place, so I had no point of reference to work from.

So I agreed to move in with Paul's parents temporarily, till we had the financial wherewithal to get a place of our own. And, that night, as we cuddled up in one of the two single beds in his childhood bedroom, despite the incongruous surroundings, it felt right. I said so and in response, Paul pulled me close to him, squeezed me tightly and whispered 'got you,' into my ear.

It *was* right. I couldn't have been happier.

CHAPTER FIVE
MOVING ON

For Paul's parents - his mother, particularly - I became the enemy very early on. It was already clear to me that she had him on something of a pedestal, but now it was becoming obvious, bit by little bit, that it was a pedestal that sat higher than any mortal could probably reach. But more specifically – and infuriatingly - it was drummed into me almost immediately, and because of the same issue we'd tussled over months previously; that of the reason why he couldn't use my car.

By now I was working at three jobs. I was still modelling more or less full time, plus helping out with the agency's office admin, and also, when I could, setting up and running casino events for Roger's growing business.

Paul, on the other hand, was back trying to get whatever work he could, while trying to plug away at his ambition to be a musician. After the security of a regular wage coming in from the Black and White Minstrel's tour, he was back to earning rather erratically, too, getting whatever work he could as an extra, either at Pinewood or Elstree studios but more often than not, on location at some stately home or other.

As with everything to do with film-making, the hours could be very anti-social, and he would often have to be on set for 5am. This meant a 4am start and naturally posed a major problem – because of his ban, he couldn't drive, so would have to work out all sorts of complex public transport options in order to get where he needed to be.

I tried to be as helpful as I could; offering to get up and drive him to the station, but he always insisted that I stay in bed and that he could easily do the 20-minute walk to the station. I wanted to do so anyway, as I was already aware that his parents found the whole business a bit odd, particularly on days when I didn't need the car myself.

'Don't you think you're being a bit selfish,' his mother challenged me one day when I wasn't starting work till later, 'making poor Paul use public transport when your car's sitting right out there? Would it be such a hardship for you to walk down and get the tube?'

Having promised Paul I would keep his secret, I had no defence to this. 'I did offer it to him,' was all I could usefully come up with. 'I told him he could use it, but he insisted I have it.'

Her response to this was to harangue me even further. 'It's not that, is it?' she challenged me. 'You just don't like him driving your car, do you? You *always* drive. You just don't trust him with it, do you?'

Again, there wasn't much I could say without revealing the truth. But I doggedly held my ground. 'That's not true.'

'Well, if that's so,' she huffed angrily, 'then you should *insist*, Vikie. Show him a little more consideration!'

Angry at being made out to be the villain of the piece, I tackled Paul about it that very night. 'You don't realise how horrible it is for me,' I told him. 'Having to live with your parents always sniping at me about it. Why can't you just *tell* them, for Gods' sake, so it's done with'.

He was having none of it, reiterating that they must never, ever know, and trying to mollify me by promising that he'd speak to them about it. 'Don't worry,' he kept saying, 'I'll put them straight about it. Reassure them. Make it clear that it's my choice and that it's fine'.

But, of course it wasn't fine, because all that did was create further discord; as soon as Paul tried to make his point his mother simply came back guns blazing. 'Then you're being much too *nice*, Paul!' she snapped. 'And *why*? Because she really doesn't deserve it!' And, of course, I overheard every word.

There was also the issue of us sleeping in the single beds. In reality we weren't, of course. We always slept in Paul's bed, which was extremely cramped and uncomfortable. But if I ever dared suggest I sleep in the other one, he'd get all upset, reading it as evidence I didn't love him as much as I used to.

His parents, in contrast, seemed to truly believe that though we were both in our late twenties and in a romantic relationship we slept in separate beds every night. So there was no question of us swapping the singles for a double – the only solution, which became apparent to me very quickly – was that we made finding our own place a big priority.

And we were in luck. In the February Paul returned from work one day with the news that an old friend of his was now working for an estate agents and that they were marketing some new flats in Barnet. 'We should go and see them,' he suggested, and I couldn't have agreed more. Though his income was sporadic, I was reasonably confident we could manage it. And I knew anything would be better than having to behave like a pair of furtive teenagers at his parents' house.

The flats were perfect - lovely, bright two-bedroomed apartments in a nice area - and we wasted no time in scraping a deposit together - the £1500 I'd saved, plus the £100 Paul managed to find - then applying for a mortgage and putting in an offer. And when it was accepted and we were able to move in, we were both ecstatic. It was the first time since we'd been together that we were properly alone.

It was an idyllic few weeks. We had almost nothing to call our own – so moving in was easy – and we couldn't have cared less. We spent the first months sitting on deckchairs and sleeping on a mattress on the floor, but we didn't mind at all. The flat had a cooker and a washing machine – what more did we need?

Money, however, was very tight. Though my modelling was going well – I could now pick and choose the best assignments – the income from the various jobs I was doing was vital, just to be sure of having enough for the mortgage. Which was fine, too – I was only too happy to support Paul in his ambitions, and with him getting more and better singing gigs now, I felt positive he'd eventually achieve them.

But it seemed there was scope for him to earn a little more in the short term as well.

The modelling agent I worked for, Nola, had by this time met Paul, and, with his good looks, felt he might have a future as a male model. No, it wasn't his ambition, but it could definitely provide a bit of extra income, and, flattered by this, Paul immediately agreed.

The only problem was that the only pictures he had currently were the rather old-fashioned, clean cut Andy Williams style ones that he used for his cabaret singing.

'We need something more up to date,' Nola told us. 'Something more sexy and relevant.' So she fixed us up to visit a photographer she knew, who'd achieve the required transformation.

Paul's hair was long at the time and he often grew his beard a little, to achieve the then-popular George Michael style stubble. It was a great look and worked well with casual T-Shirts and leather jackets, and he looked just as great clean-shaven for some more formal ones, wearing a suit.

The pictures were so good, in fact, that I was gobsmacked. And so was Paul. He was clearly a natural and couldn't have been more excited when he saw them. This was just the image change he needed and we both felt very positive about it. His own agent was always on to him about bringing his act up to date. So, who knew? It might even help his singing career.

He was, however, strangely reluctant to show them to his parents.

'But they'll love them!' I insisted as we drove there the following Sunday, the finished portfolio of photos in the back seat. 'You look fantastic,' I added, wondering why he was so anxious about them seeing them. 'How could they not like them? You look so good!'

I soon was to find out. We were over for a Sunday roast, which was something of an institution in the family. Though Paul's younger brother Peter had long since moved out (he was married and he and his wife lived a couple of miles away) Paul's parents still did a traditional full roast, round the table, every weekend, with all the usual bells and whistles – always the best china and cutlery – with the Hostess Trolley always ready in the corner. Paul's mum, too – at least, to look at – was similarly unremarkable. On the short side, around four foot ten, and always well turned out, if you passed her on the street you'd notice nothing untoward.

But, as far as normality went, that's where it ended. There was clearly something very far from normal going on within those spotless chintzy walls. We'd just finished eating and were now milling around, clearing the table, when Paul's mother asked him to go and fetch the photos, us having already mentioned them over lunch. So he went to get them and even as he pulled them from the envelope, I realised he was really quite concerned about both his parents' reactions because he was already telling them they were unlike any he'd had done before.

And as reactions went, it was really quite astonishing. Paul's mum said nothing – instead, she immediately burst into tears and rushed off into the kitchen, Paul and his father in pursuit.

I was gobsmacked. I couldn't quite believe what I'd seen. These were fashion photos, that was all. Everyday model agency photos. Yet, Paul's mother had reacted in such an extreme distraught fashion. What about them could possibly have upset her so much?

I wasn't long getting an answer. And quite forcefully, too. She came back in a few moments later, followed by Paul and his father again, furious. And the object of her fury was me. 'How dare you!' she screamed at me. 'You had no right to do this! You're a terrible influence – an *evil* influence – on our son!'

It was difficult to know what to say to that accusation, apart from pointing out that it hadn't been my idea to get them done, which I did. 'But what's wrong with them anyway?' I tried to ask her. 'They're really good. He looks great.'

'Great?' she screeched. 'Great! You have *completely* sexualised him! They're horrible. They're disgusting! They're obscene!' She paused only to catch her breath, the tears spilling onto her cheeks. 'You,' she cried, 'have completely destroyed his innocence!'

Now I was as speechless as she had been when she'd seen the photos. He was *29 years old* – what 'innocence' was she referring to? And they weren't remotely pornographic anyway - they were perfectly normal pictures by anyone's yardstick – the sort of pictures you'd see in any fashion magazine. Yet they had reduced what had at first sight seemed a perfectly normal woman to rant and rave hysterically, and her perfectly normal husband – who clearly wasn't that either – to go on and on about them for the rest of the afternoon.

Predictably, Paul's reaction to all this was bizarre. Despite his mother's ranting at me being inappropriate and, to my mind, indefensible, he did try to defend them, hard. He was also apologising for them, over and over and over, as if, in agreeing to the pictures, he'd been caught out committing some heinous crime. Which, astoundingly, they seemed to think he - or more correctly, *I* had. At one point they even had to go out into the garden so they could be alone to discuss the enormity of it privately.

We left for home eventually (there being no point in staying) Paul irritable, me dazed and confused. Had I *really* witnessed what I just thought I'd witnessed? And once we were home, there was a second turnaround. Paul now wasted no time lambasting them for it; ranting on furiously, just like his mother had a couple of hours earlier, about how narrow-minded they were and how angry he was at their reaction.

None of which he'd said to their faces. Which made me feel more confused than ever, because I'd seen him go at his parents like a rabid dog more than once, over 'old chestnuts' I knew nothing about – them being before my time - swearing and shouting at them and reducing his mother to tears, and on at least one occasion, almost coming to blows with his father. I'd never seen anything quite like it; I'd never have dared speak to my parents in such a way, but they never retaliated – just let him bully them into submission. I couldn't get my head around the bizarre nature of their family dynamic at all.

It was all beginning to fit a pattern, however. A pattern that I should have seen and been concerned about. Shortly after that, Paul was offered some work in a pantomime, which he didn't want to accept. After faffing around for ages, too scared to call his agent and tell him, he eventually got his mum to do it for him.

'You did what?' I asked astonished, when I came home from work and he confessed to this. I was cross, because money was tight and I was working all hours, so he should have taken the work. But I was even crosser, especially after the incident with the photos, that he'd acted like a child of nine instead of a man of almost 30. 'How could you do that?' I railed at him. 'Why on earth couldn't you have done that yourself? How can you be so scared of saying no to someone that you can't even pick up a phone?'

'You know I don't like confrontation,' he replied. *No, not unless it's with me*, I thought. 'And what's your problem anyway? She has much more free time to do it than I do, and if she doesn't mind doing it, why *shouldn't* she make the call?'

'Because she shouldn't,' I told him, stupefied by his inability to understand that it wasn't acceptable for a grown man to have his mum make his excuses. 'Just because you don't enjoy doing it,' I tried to explain, 'that doesn't mean you shouldn't *do* it. It's not adult. You need to be doing these things yourself.'

But my words obviously fell on deaf ears because the same thing happened a few weeks later, when he had to cancel a dental check up because of some work. He asked me to do it for him first and I came back straight away with the fact that I wasn't going to do such a simple thing for him just because he didn't like the thought of it. 'Once you start doing it,' I said, trying to get him to see why it mattered, 'you'll find it so much easier to do it the next time.'

'No I won't,' he responded. 'You know I hate doing that sort of thing. You should support me. But that's fine. If you won't do it then I'll get mum to instead.' Then, with a demeanour that put me in mind of a defiant schoolboy, he proceeded to do exactly that.

Once again, I was stunned, but also angry. I phoned his mother straight back and asked her how she thought doing so was helping, and that she should make Paul stand up and be a man – not a mouse. This enraged her – how dare I call her precious son a mouse! And how dare I make such a big thing out of nothing!

'But it's *not* nothing!' I said. 'It's extremely important. This might just be a little thing but if he can't even manage that much, what happens when there's a really *big* thing he has to deal with?'

They were words that would come back and haunt me decades later, but for now all I could think was that I was perpetually having to fight against someone who had only one goal in her life – to stop her son from ever having to face the tiniest amount of stress and inconvenience and – worse – making it clear that my role was to do the same. He was her son and she would always be his mother, and would do absolutely *anything* to make him happy. And as far as she was concerned that was my remit as well. If I truly loved him, that was.

And it was a philosophy that had not served Paul well. One night, after a party, we had Paul's friend Steve back to stay and I was to be aghast again at how that was my apparent role in his life too. We all sat and talked long into the night, the boys both drinking quite heavily, and dawn was break- ing when Paul casually suggested, in front of Steve, that it would be nice if I went to bed with both of them.

I couldn't believe what I was hearing. I was shocked to the core that he could even suggest such a thing. But he was deadly serious. Requests soon turned into demands and, perhaps inevitably, given that there'd been so much drink involved, he became violent, ending up by trapping me in the bathroom and ripping my dressing gown off me, leaving it in several pieces on the floor. I was heartbroken by that because the dressing gown was one of the few things I had left that had belonged to my mother. I managed to escape to bed then, naked and terrified and bruised all over, and wondering how the man who professed to love me so much could be so cruel.

Surely I had to leave him, I kept telling myself over the coming days. How could I survive in a relationship with someone so unpredictable? Whose mood could change so dramatically from one moment to the next? Who seemed to need to take everything that went wrong in his life out on me?

Yet how could I leave him? That was what vexed me the most. I still had such strong feelings for him, despite everything, and our lives were now completely entangled financially, as well – so what about the flat? We'd made a home together and the thought of unravelling everything so soon after doing that filled me with something like dread. He'd be better surely once he was away from his mother's influence; he'd be *so* much better. Perhaps I should hang on to that.

But it wasn't the insecurity, or the complexity. These were all just excuses. Yes, it might have been my fractured childhood that made me so keen for us to stick together, but the truth was that I loved him.

Despite his flaws, I was still *in* love with him. So I was determined to make it work.

Chapter Six

'YOU NEED TO CHANGE'

It seemed to me that one of the best things I could do for Paul was to put every ounce of energy I could into helping him realise his singing ambitions. I believed in him. He had charisma, a beautiful voice and lots of musical talent. Surely if we put our all into it, I reasoned, there was a chance for him to hit the big time.

And, on the face of it, he was extremely well placed to. For starters, he had some decent contacts within the industry. Joan Armatrading's brother, Tony, was a friend and sometimes visitor to our flat, and various of his other friends were in the industry or fellow musicians. I would spend long hours with them, trying to enthuse them to form a proper band, rather than just sitting around in the flat, 'jamming'. I also tried several times to get them to put together a demo tape, but there was a level of apathy that was frankly bewildering. So much talk about doing this, that or the other – yet so little ever translated to action. I got this sense that they were just sitting around waiting for someone to discover them – hardly likely, when they never made any music outside the flat!

But then, out of the blue, there seemed to come a break. Paul had long had a contact called Eric Hall, who had been a big noise in the music scene for over a decade. He was something of a 'super-agent', having worked with the likes of Paul McCartney and Queen and also Elton John, who was a personal friend. He'd also worked with the notorious punk band, the Sex Pistols, being the person credited with arranging their infamous appearance on the Today Show. If anyone could propel Paul into stardom, it was him, and when we managed to secure a meeting with him in the summer of 1985, we couldn't have been more excited.

Paul asked me to go along with him, and we turned up at Eric's house in Central London tingling with anticipation. This could be the turning point in both our lives. And once we started chatting it was clear that he believed in Paul's talent too; then and there he said he'd take Paul on, much to my delight, and started talking about demo tapes, studio time and which record label might be best. There was only one proviso; just as I'd suspected since back when we'd done the fashion photo shoot with Nola, he wanted Paul to change his image.

Eric felt Paul was very much in the Tony Hadley mould – the charismatic front man of the band Spandau Ballet - and wanted him to update his whole look from one that was rather old-fashioned and 'wholesome' to something more flamboyant and dramatic. Which I understood; this was the time of the New Romantics and Band Aid – a time of real musical and stylistic innovation, and Paul's look, which was stuck in that 70's David

Cassidy mould, was just completely out of step for the times.

Straight away however, to my dismay, he began arguing with Eric.

'Why do I need to do that?' he asked, and I could immediately hear the edge in his voice.

Eric looked shocked as well. He'd clearly never dreamt that Paul would object to such a thing. 'To look more current,' he offered, diplomatically. 'I'm not talking about doing anything radical. Just updating your hair and look to fit in with the competition.'

'But I don't *want* to fit in,' Paul countered. 'I want to be myself. I want it to be all about me as a person and my music.'

'It *is* all about that,' Eric said. 'Of course it's about that. Which is why it's really no big deal to change the packaging a bit, surely? It's cosmetic – no one's trying to change what you're doing as a musician. I just want you to look more marketable, that's all.'

He seemed bemused by Paul more than anything, and at that point, happy enough to humour him. But Paul seemed determined to change bemusement to opposition, digging his heels in as deeply as he could. 'I don't want to be "more marketable",' he shot back. 'I want people to accept me for the musician I *am*. Not some construct that isn't really me.'

Eric considered. 'Look, Paul,' he said finally. 'Here's the way it has to work. I can't help you if you're not prepared to change the way you look. And to be honest, if you're already so resistant to something so relatively small, how are you going to be when it comes to something that *is* important?'

I winced at that 'is'. Because I knew Eric was right. It was Paul's way or no way. Which in this case meant no way. He'd left Eric little choice but to deliver the standard, damning line. 'Well, if you change your mind, Paul, you know where I am.'

Needless to say, once we were home we had an almighty row. I couldn't believe that he was prepared to throw away the biggest chance he'd ever been offered, and he wouldn't budge – not an inch. Was it simply arrogance? If so, it was serving him very badly. I also felt furious that he was so entrenched in his position that he wouldn't even try to meet Eric – who knew so much about the business than Paul did – at least halfway. Or was it something deeper; was it just as I'd seen at our meeting? That there was never going to be any halfway point with Paul? No grey areas. No compromise. You were either with him or you were against him - something that would become so much clearer to me later down the line.

Right then, however, I was all out of energy for fighting. This was the biggest investment of professional time and interest Paul had ever received and I couldn't believe he was prepared to throw it in Eric's face just because he didn't want to modernise his look. And though Eric had at least left the door open for him to change his mind and get his career rejuvenated, I knew that no amount of cajoling on my part would shift him. So that was that. I gave up trying to help him with his 'dream' from that day on, and I think we both knew then that his singing career was over. He wasn't getting any younger and, though he still had the odd singing gig in pubs, his musical career was effectively over and instead he started working with me and Roger.

If Paul's dreams of fame and fortune had once been grounded in the possible, in other areas of life I was beginning to realise he was an archetypal daydreamer. Since I'd known him, I'd continued to work long hours every week, not out of martyrdom, but simply because I knew no other way to be. There was a mortgage that needed paying, so I just got on with it. Paul, on the other hand, seemed locked in a state of stasis – still waiting for the big career break that would see him doing the job he felt he *should* be – a break that, now he'd refused Eric's representation, seemed increasingly unlikely would ever come. Yes, he put the hours in whenever work as an extra, or the increasingly infrequent gig, came his way, but he seemed unable to accept the reality that he needed to find an alternative career.

Emotionally, life had plateaued into what seemed to be our 'normal'. Either Paul was happy, in which case, things were wonderful between us, or he was not, and it was like living in hell. The slightest thing could make him snap and when he did I certainly knew about it. Today, of course, the word 'bipolar' might well spring straight to mind, but back then, except for in the minds of a few medical professionals, that now-familiar expression didn't even exist, so it never occurred to me that Paul might have mental health issues. I just thought he was different from me.

Though just how different, I was yet to find out.

Just as with the death of Kennedy, and, latterly, that of Princess Diana, an awful lot of people of a certain age know where they were and what they were doing on the day of the Live Aid concerts in London and Philadelphia. We were no exception. We were in our flat, watching the whole thing, accompanied by our brand new kitten, Sunny, who we'd collected from the local pet shop that very morning.

I hadn't been at all keen on getting a cat – we lived in a flat, after all, which meant it would have to be kept indoors all the time. Plus I was a 'dog' person, if it came down to a straight choice. But Paul was a 'cat' person and when he got a bee in his bonnet it was almost a foregone conclusion; he had this way of chipping away at me, of having an answer to every objection, of weakening my resolve to such an extent that he invariably got his way in the end.

And in this case, I conceded he was right. There was something so wonderful about having a little life to take care of and, despite my being just about as non-maternal as you could get, I loved coming home to him at the end of the working day.

'But we need another,' Paul announced a few days after we got him. 'He'll be lonely when we're both out at work – it's not fair on him.' So, despite my misgivings (and weren't cats solitary animals anyway?) back we went to the pet shop to pick up a second kitten, Dizzy – a gorgeous little tabby that immediately melted my heart, and who seemed to get on with Sunny straight away.

Unfortunately, they got on a little too well. Paul point blank refused to have either kitten neutered, on the grounds that it was unnatural and cruel, so it was only a matter of time before the inevitable happened and we came home one night to find our numbers had swelled – she'd given birth to four kittens of her own.

No matter, I thought. We'd have no trouble selling the kittens and now that Dizzy had had a litter, it seemed reasonable to have her neutered. It was the responsible thing to do, after all. But once again, Paul was having none of it.

'It's just not natural,' he kept repeating. 'And we can't get rid of the kittens either. What about Dizzy and Sunny? It's not fair on them.'

I tried to point out that cats letting go of their kittens was, actually, perfectly natural, and that there was also the small issue of feeding and toileting – one being ridiculously expensive and the other a constant domestic trial. And one that would only become more icky, I knew, once we had six fully-grown animals in the flat.

In the end, he was persuaded to get Dizzy neutered at least. I kept banging on about how bad it would be for her to have another litter so soon, and that we couldn't possibly cope with having ten cats in the flat. Grudgingly, he eventually agreed to have her spayed, just before she was due to be in season once again.

I was profoundly relieved. Though I loved the cats, it was insane that we had even let things ride that far. It was also perhaps a hint I should have taken heed of; it would be repeated with creating a human family later. But as it was a family I had no idea I was capable of creating, it wasn't something that even crossed my mind.

With six feline mouths to feed, not to mention the vet's bills, our domestic reality was that we were increasingly strapped for cash. But along came another break – one that revealed a potential new career, utilising a talent we didn't realise Paul even had.

By now I was working for Roger's games business pretty much full time. I loved the work, I loved the travelling, and I loved the buzz of putting events on, so that the business was expanding so fast was all to the good. But it was entirely by chance that Paul began to get involved. It was down to our usual chronic cash-flow problems in fact; I mentioned that Paul had no work on and Roger responded by telling me he'd happily pay him to go and sort out his warehouse.

Roger rented office and warehouse space in Pinner, just outside London, using one half of a converted barn that was the premises of an entertainment agent he knew. This was the hub of his own burgeoning business, and the place where I worked when not on the road.

Roger was an energetic and inspiring boss but he was hopelessly disorganised, so the warehouse – the part Paul was ask to sort out – was nothing short of chaotic. There was stuff all over the place, with no system and everything flung together, and much of the equipment in a poor state of repair – something a couple of clients had even remarked upon.

And Paul was the right man for the job. I had long since learned that he was tidy to the point of obsession. Despite our six cats, the flat was never less than spick and span and he kept everything organisable organised to the extreme. This didn't just take the form of arranging his

CDs in alphabetical order, either. Paul arranged everything with minute precision. His whole life seemed to be recorded on index cards, which were stored in a box he made himself so that it fitted them exactly, and every pen and pencil on his desk was laid equidistant to every other, with any writing on the side facing up. He also copied out every song lyric he'd ever written, on A4 paper, which he protected in plastic pockets, and had them organised in colour-coded ring binders. Not terribly rock and roll.

Needless to say, it was like a whirlwind had blown through the warehouse when Roger and I cast our eyes over what Paul had done, three days later, even I – who was used to Paul's obsession with order – was gobsmacked by how much he'd achieved in so short a space of time.

And he didn't finish there. 'I could renovate all this equipment for you if you like,' he suggested, and Roger, goggle-eyed seeing the transformation Paul had already wrought, was quick to take him up on the offer.

It was another skill Paul had perhaps never really realised he had and, best of all, really seemed to enjoy. Before long, every piece of equipment looked brand new and he also built some new games, such as Splat the Rat, from scratch. All in all it was such a boost to the business that Roger asked him to work for him full time.

It was the start of an incredibly fruitful period. Though Paul's obsession with order was another thing that would eventually come to dominate our lives, at the time it felt as if he'd finally found a way to make a living that made him happy, which made me happy too. And with all three of us working now, the business started growing even faster and, in relationship terms, that was good for us as well. With Roger, Paul and I all charging up and down the country to various events, we were suddenly seeing rather less of one another, which made our relationship so much less intense. It all felt much healthier, and with Paul contributing more financially now, the pressure on funds disappeared too.

Most importantly, it meant we had so much less opportunity to argue, so I forgot all about my misgivings and concerns about whether I should stay with him. Yes, we still had the odd blazing row about nothing, but with Paul occupied and earning, instead of chasing dreams, I realised this was what we'd needed all along.

But it was to be a purple patch of short duration. One rare day, when all three of us were working in the office, Roger came in with what would turn out to be some life-changing news.

'I've decided we need to move the business to the Midlands,' he announced. Then, presumably seeing the look on my face, added, 'I have no choice, Vikie; my wife needs to be nearer her mother. Will you come with me?'

Paul was immediately keen, but, for me, the short answer was no. 'I'm not leaving London,' I said, and I meant it. London was the place I'd chosen to call home when I was still in my teens and I was adamant I'd live there and die there. I'd also vowed that if I was forced to move, kicking and screaming, nothing could have ever made me relocate to the Midlands.

'I can offer you a really good financial package,' Roger persisted. 'I know it's an upheaval, but I've been thinking, and how about I upped your salaries and gave you a cut of the profits as well? That would at least give you a bit more of an incentive.'

I didn't feel remotely incentivised, however. It wasn't about money. It was about living where I wanted to live. What could possibly entice me to head for the Black Country when, compared to London, it was a cultural desert? No, if Roger was off to the Midlands, it would be without me. I was adamant. If he couldn't find a way to make it work with us staying down in London, then we would have to part company. I wasn't going to budge.

CHAPTER SEVEN
INTO THE WILD

Paul was enthusiastic about moving to the Midlands from the off, so I suppose I should have realised that he'd get straight to work on me, and not stop until he'd succeeded in changing my mind. Once it was settled that there was no chance of us continuing working in London, he seemed as determined about 'organising' me into his way of thinking as he had about stamping his personality on Roger's warehouse. To that end he kept coming home with details of admittedly beautiful properties he'd found for us, and badgering me to go and see them with him.

'I don't know why you keep on doing this,' I snapped at him one evening, when he was chipping away at me once again, with this house and that house. 'You'll never do it,' I said. 'Really, Paul, you will *never* find a property incredible enough to persuade me to move away from London. *Never.*'

It took him only another week to do just that.

In fact, we went to see a bungalow first, in a little village called Hatton. The village was very chocolate boxy, but I immediately felt ill at ease. The vendors were much older than us and the property itself was surrounded by other similar bungalows, doubtless occupied by sweet but equally mature couples. Everything seemed to suggest that, from the well-tended gardens and neatly parked cars to the net curtains that shrouded every window. In fact the whole place had a feeling of sleepy middle-aged contentment, which made me feel almost desperate to run away. Just the idea of living so far away from the beating heart of a city traumatised me. I could feel the space, the big blue sky, not as an indicator of freedom but as a beautiful but suffocating aerial cloak; one that I knew would close in and snuff the life out of me.

But I hadn't reckoned on the next house Paul broached as a must-see. It was the beginning of July, and a perfect summer's day. They always say that you should view a property in the worst possible weather, so that if you still love it, you'll know you chose well. It's so easy to be beguiled – even hoodwinked – by glorious weather, after all.

But I don't think it would have made any difference what the weather had been doing. Nor the fact that, this being in the days before Sat Nav was invented, we got so hopelessly lost trying to find the place. Paul, being a typical man, refused to ask anyone for directions, either, so, in the end, being an hour late for our appointment by now, it was left to me to jump out and use the next phone box we spotted, to ring and apologise and let them know we were on our way.

And as we made our final approach, I felt so differently already. There was no sleepy-looking community here – just a picturesque lane, flanked by what looked like miles of woodland. It wasn't exactly that I ever felt that 'hell was other people' but if we were heading into the wild, I wanted it to be properly wild. It would feel so much more like an adventure, that way.

And on arrival, it did nothing to dampen my quiet (and unexpected) feeling of positivity. It was the sort of home that, like a supermodel, would have looked good whatever the circumstance, that would sit just as prettily in a brooding, charcoal-skied storm, would look just as charming tipped with hoar frost or raked by a howling gale.

But, of course, lit by a setting sun on a balmy summer evening, it was definitely showing us its best side.

The house itself was somewhat rambling - definitely nothing like as sleek as a super-model - and once we got inside, it was migraine-inducing territory, as the lovely owners had a passion for pattern that seemed to know no bounds. Nothing was spared; walls and carpets, furnishings and soft furnishings – even the lampshades hadn't escaped from the application of chintzy prints.

But that didn't seem to matter, because, suddenly, I could see potential everywhere - for all its lack of ambition in terms of designer pzazz, it sat in 13 acres of glorious rural land and came with an established livery business, to boot – something that would provide a valuable income that could help pay for the massive mortgage we'd be saddled with. It was also blessed with everything it needed to suggest a rural idyll; the neat paddocks were obviously accessorised with horses and ponies and there were chickens clucking as they strutted around the stable yard. It was so beautiful, in short, that even I fell in love with the dream.

And Paul could obviously tell he'd hit the spot. He was like a man possessed during the lengthy journey home, seizing on my 'well, if I had to move, this would definitely be the sort of place I'd be prepared to move to' as evidence that he had a done deal.

And yes, I did like it, and yes, I had fallen for the ponies and chickens aspect, but the next morning – we'd gone to separate locations for work that day – I was concerned that he was already badgering me about putting in an offer. In the end, I relented; I had already been talked round the previous evening, after all. But then he went and did something astonishing. I came home from work that night, late and tired, to find that he'd indeed made 'an offer'. For the full – and financially perilous – asking price.

'You did what?' I asked, aghast. And I was aghast, too. The house wasn't an easy sell, and had been on the market for some time. It was remote, would need a lot of work and – the most salient point – was also very close to a mine there was talk of being opened in a place called Berkswell, which would mean reopening a railway track that ran only 100 yards from the house. These vendors, I knew, would probably have bitten our hands off at a much lower price; particularly as the lady had a back injury and really needed to move to somewhere more suitable sooner rather than later.

But this evidently hadn't figured in Paul's thinking.

'Well, we have to retract it,' I said, thinking on my feet. That's what we'll do. God, Paul, why on *earth* didn't you negotiate with them? We had a golden opportunity to get it really reasonably – why didn't you *think*?'

'That's easy for you to say,' he snapped back. 'And I did think, as it happens. But why risk it? Suppose I did that and they refused to sell it to us?'

'Why on earth would they do that?' I argued, feeling the frustration rising in me.

'Because,' he snapped back, as if I was missing something fundamental, 'they'll probably think we're taking the piss! And then someone else would come along, and that would be that, wouldn't it?'

'*Who* else?' I wanted to know. 'It's been on the market for months!'

I was stunned – how could he be so naïve and impulsive? What the hell was the matter with him? How could he be so domineering at home with me but not be able to say boo to a goose out in the world? It made no sense at all. And he kept on, of course, egged on by both Roger and his parents. I was under no circumstances to jeopardise the purchase of what he felt was a bargain, even at the asking price, and though I knew it was all because he'd been too timid to negotiate, I promised I wouldn't. It was ridiculous, but even as I fumed about the money he might have lost us, the house was already calling to me, pulling me towards it, somehow.

'Okay,' I said eventually, 'It's done now so I suppose that's that. But on one condition, and I'm really not going to budge on this one. I'm not moving somewhere so isolated without getting a dog. A *big* dog.'

Paul agreed in a heartbeat.

We moved on the 12th December 1986, on one of those dark, depressing, murky winter's days that make you long for spring, even as you've just finished autumn. Though not before I'd headed off to Battersea Dogs Home to find the promised dog while Paul and his father finished loading up the borrowed company van.

Choosing the right animal was an important decision. Having been unable to have a dog in London, I was excited about the prospect, but there would be no compromise - it had to be the right one.

I'd been to Battersea Dog's Home when I was 20, to pick out a dog for my father once, and it was no less heartbreaking now than it had been then. Rows and rows of dogs looking up at me, beseeching me to take a shine to them, some leaping up with their tails wagging hopefully, others more timid, gazing up with big, sad, soulful eyes. I wanted to take all of them, but at the same time none quite suited. I was looking for that connection, and I knew I'd know when I saw it.

But by the time we got to the last few enclosures I'd already steeled myself a little, realising I might have to come back on a different day. But then we reached a cage which housed two dogs rather than the usual one; a German Shepherd, who was cowering at the rear of the enclosure, and a cross-breed, who was already barking excitedly, and who the kennel maid said she felt sure was German Shepherd mixed with some kind of bulldog.

'We think they're mother and daughter,' she explained. 'They came in together and we'd like them to be re-homed together as well. Though it's not looking easy. The cross here is very relaxed and friendly, as you can see, but the mum won't let anyone get near her. It's both or neither, though,' she added. 'We don't feel we can separate them.'

I didn't want two dogs, but I was drawn in even so. There was something about the way the German Shepherd was looking at me that made me connect with her, even though she was stationed at the back of the cage, looking very wary.

'Can I go in anyway?' I asked the girl.

'Course you can,' she said, unlocking the door. 'But be careful,' she added as I stepped inside. 'No one's been able to get near her in three weeks and she's unpredictable. She'll either cower right away or start growling at you. And if she does that, please don't approach her.'

I sat down close to the door, with my back to the mesh and as I'd anticipated, the younger dog was all over me. The older one, however, remained at the back, with her eyes trained on me, but as she neither cowered or growled I decided there was no harm in seeing how she'd react if I moved to the back of the cage.

I did so, squatting down and then sitting directly onto the concrete, upon which, to my surprise and delight, she walked the couple of feet towards me, then flopped down beside me, very close.

'Wow,' I mouthed to the kennel maid, who gave me a two-handed thumbs up as I risked placing an arm across the bitch's back. The response wasn't only gratifying, it was a real defining moment; she immediately nestled her head against the side of my chest, as if I was the person she'd been waiting to come and visit her all her life, and that, now I'd arrived she could finally go home.

I am not remotely superstitious, nor do I believe in psychics, but to have an animal respond to me in that way felt surreal. It was a sign, surely? This dog and I *did* have a connection. I didn't know why, but I didn't care - that was an irrelevance. Paul would be furious but I decided then and there. I was going to take both of them home. And if he complained I'd simply throw his own kitten logic back at him – that we needed two so they'd be company for one another.

I called the German Shepherd Dawn, to signify the dawning of a new life for her and, once introduced to her daughter, Paul, whose predictable anger had abated quickly, soon named the other one Spring. Which was certainly apt because, so excited by being uncaged at last, she could – and often would – spring several feet into the air, much to the amusement of everyone who saw her.

For now, though, we had new lives of our own to get organised, and, what with my trip to Battersea Dogs home and the distance we had to travel, it was almost ten before we finally arrived, with six cats and the two dogs in tow. Tired and frazzled, getting something to eat was a priority, so I was dispatched to get food – any kind of food, from anywhere – while Paul pressed on with unpacking the essentials so we could at least get a decent night's sleep.

This proved easier said than done, as I could barely work out how to get to the nearest town – Kenilworth – let alone find somewhere I could perhaps pick up a takeaway. I got lost several times before eventually finding a Chinese restaurant in the town centre, which, by the look of it, was still open for business. Not that there were many signs of life. This was a Friday evening, but could equally have been Sunday, it was so deathly quiet.

Quelling the feelings of dismay – could I really live so far away from bustle and life and takeaways? – I parked in one of the bays at the side of the road and went inside. It was a shabby modern place which looked incongruous set among the beautiful old buildings that surrounded it. And though there was a television blaring in the corner and the sound of activity out back, there was no one out front actually serving.

I stood for a few moments, lightly coughing to make my presence felt, when a woman suddenly burst through the bead curtain behind the counter, a very large woman, a very obviously Chinese woman. Which was the clue that made my stupidity unforgivable.

'Way wan!' she greeted me.

'Um, I'd like to order a takeaway, if that's okay?' I answered.

She nodded towards the counter itself, on which there was a large takeaway menu under glass.

'Way wan!' she said again.

'I'm sorry?' I said, perusing the menu.

'Way *wan*?' she said again, this time making it clear that it was a question.

'Um...' I began.

'Way *wan*?' she said a fourth time, tapping a finger against the menu.

The penny dropped then. She was saying '*what do you want?*'!

I could feel a blush creeping up my neck as I relayed my brief order. What must she think of me? I must have come across as being so ignorant. What a terrible way to make acquaintance with one of the locals, particularly since this might be the only takeaway for miles. Still, I thought, forgiving myself – I was dog-tired, after all – it would be at least something funny to share with Paul once I brought the food home. Way wan. How idiotic was I?

In the event, though, it was such a long, dispiriting journey home that by the time I got there all thoughts of telling my little anecdote had evaporated. Everyone knew the expression 'living in the middle of nowhere' but here I was, actually about to *really* live it. All of a sudden, I could no longer see any positives to being in this place - bar the dogs, Dawn particularly, who greeted my return as if I was a long lost lover. The dark was just so dark, the sky so vast, the night so eerie and silent. I wanted dustcarts and midnight revellers, I wanted streams of cars and buses. I wanted light-pollution, neon signage, *life*.

We had none, and as we sat and ate our first meal together, I felt horribly, scarily alone.

Chapter Eight
CHICKEN RUN!

December was an incredibly busy month for Roger's business, and with the diary full of office Christmas parties and other festive business gatherings, Paul and I were like ships that passed in the night for much of the time, and we didn't really have time to get settled in.

Not that we had a great deal *to* settle. We had moved into a large four-bedroom house in 13 acres of land and our worldly goods in their entirety fitted easily into a van. How that would change over the coming years – to an extent I could never have imagined – but right then, even with the dogs and cats, we really were rattling around in the place. By the time the season to be jolly came around we'd barely been inside half the rooms, let alone made them remotely habitable.

Christmas came and went – tensely, as we'd had both my father and his girlfriend and Paul's parents to stay; a volatile mix – but with the new year came the promise of getting properly orientated in our new lives, when Roger moved the business hub to the new house he'd bought in nearby Rugby. It was a large house – larger than ours – and came with plenty of renovated stables in which to house all the equipment and provide space for the office.

Though space wasn't the reason we'd made the move to the Midlands – that had been Roger's mother in law – there was no doubt that, away from London, we were also well-located to expand the business across a greater part of the country, and having agreed to the move I was beginning to feel more positive about getting stuck in. We were, after all, ridiculously busy, so there was no reason to feel anything else.

I was about to get a very rude awakening.

It was on a dull drizzly morning in February when Roger called us both into the office, a little like our collective spirits. After the pre-Christmas madness, January had been extremely quiet, but as that was to be expected, I wasn't unduly concerned. It would pick up again soon, I knew, once spring was in the offing. It was a seasonal kind of business to some extent, after all.

Even so, there'd been something of a strained atmosphere in the office lately, which I'd put down to stress following the move and it being January, but as we went into the office, something told me might be more. 'I'm not going to beat around the bush,' he said, having done exactly that for a good 15 minutes or so, 'but I've got a bit of a cash flow problem.'

This wasn't really news. There was always a bit of a timelag between putting on an event and the company settling the invoice, and Roger wasn't the most organised of people. Yes, he owed us quite a lot of money – some

£15,000 by now, in fact, as we'd let it run for a bit so that he could invest in advertising and equipment. But, given his move to his lovely new house, and the fact that, despite the January lull, we'd had a hugely successful autumn and winter, I had no reason to doubt that now we were up here, he'd sort it all out. After all, he wouldn't bring us all this way without knowing he could afford to do so, would he? Not given the crippling mortgage he knew we'd taken on based on the financial deal he'd struck to get us to move.

Apparently yes. Not only was he not in a position to pay us what he already owed us in event fees and office time, he was now trying to renegotiate that very deal.

'I have no choice,' he said, flatly, after he ran through the reality that the increased fees and an agreed percentage of profits that had been factors in our financial planning were, as of that moment, no more. Instead we'd be back on our old rate, there were apparently no profits to have a share of, and what he could offer us in terms of unpaid fees was a joke.

I did some sums in my head. 'But that's not fair!' I said, aghast. 'That'll only give us half the income you promised us! We've just uprooted ourselves and moved 100 miles up the motorway, and you're seriously asking us to just accept that? How the hell are we supposed to pay next month's mortgage?'

'I don't know,' he admitted. 'But I don't know what else to say to you. The money's just not there. It will be – eventually – but right now I just don't have it.'

'Then find it!' Paul thundered, in an unexpected burst of assertiveness. 'You can't just backtrack on everything we've agreed!'

But of course he could. We were young and naïve and we were now going to have to pay for it. We'd not even thought to demand contracts. We were screwed.

We returned home that night shell shocked and furious. And as the dogs greeted us with their usual loving enthusiasm, I reflected that if we didn't pull a rabbit out of a hat, we'd even struggle with the eight animal mouths we had to feed. We had both believed Roger to be a man of principle and now he'd torn the rug from under us, we had completely lost our trust in him. I felt he must have known his situation was potentially precarious long before he broke the news to us and if that wasn't the case, well, that spoke volumes too. To have so much business and to be in such a financial mess didn't say a great deal for his business acumen.

We talked long into the night and by the morning had made our decision. We needed to cut our ties with Roger completely and do something else. But what? The following few weeks saw us trying to come up with ideas, and in talks with our still very patient bank manager.

We'd come up with one idea that appealed to both of us – to open a craft shop of some sort – but the answer from the bank was a swift and very definite no. Craft shops had apparently got the highest failure rate of almost any business (because they were run by whimsical fantasists like we appeared to be?) and without the bank's support we were scuppered anyway; we didn't have the funds to go it alone, even if Roger miraculously paid us everything he owed us.

No, the logical thing was to set up a fun casino and event business similar to Roger's and though it felt ethically wrong to me, the bank were very keen to support us in doing so. It was a growing sector, so there was plenty of business out there to be had and, most compelling of all, we had experience of doing it and Paul could make a lot of the necessary equipment himself.

Roger, predictably, was livid. I didn't expect him to respond differently, but he also knew the truth – that if he hadn't put us in the position he had I wouldn't have countenanced doing what we did in a million years. As it was, we had the bank's support and a means to establish some financial security, and Paul set about building the equipment in earnest. Just as we could have predicted, his meticulous attention to detail and pathological perfectionism meant that his casino tables were not only better looking than Roger's, they even looked more professional than the professional ones I used to use during my time as a croupier.

It wasn't the ideal way to start our new lives in the country and, needless to say, it put an extra strain on an already strained relationship. But, somehow, dealing with Paul's temper, and the volatile nature of our interactions had become strangely normal, especially now we had Dawn. I'd chosen both dogs, of course, and since Paul still had his fear of them, they were essentially mine, but where Spring loved every living thing – Paul included – Dawn was a different pet altogether. She was loyal to me only; she had no interest in being petted by anyone else, and, more to the point, she was incredibly protective of me.

It was now becoming apparent, as we soldiered on, trying to sort our new lives out, that if Paul so much as raised his voice to me, she wasn't happy. Her hackles would rise and, if he seemed even remotely threatening, she'd growl at him and bare her teeth.

If he was wary of her when I'd brought her home, now he was doubly nervous around her, and with good reason as well. One night, after we'd gone to bed we heard a noise out in the lane. It was around midnight and it sounded like a car pulling up – a very rare event, even in the middle of the day.

As our bedroom window looked out onto the lane, I jumped out of bed to see who it was, and, as I expected, I saw a car parked on our verge. It was hard to make out how many people were in it, but as they were parked on our property, my natural instinct was to go downstairs and see what they were doing there. Ignoring Paul's insistence that I should ignore it – he was convinced they might be dangerous – I duly went downstairs, with Dawn and Spring close beside me. Not that I was concerned. They might well just be lost. I just wanted to find out who they were and what they were doing there.

Which I found out as soon as I opened the front door, in the shape of a young man who had now got out of the car and was urinating up the trunk of our willow tree.

Cross – what a cheek! – I called out to him. 'What the hell d'you think you're doing?' I shouted across, while holding tight to Dawn's collar. She'd have been out of the door like a shot otherwise.

'I was only having a piss!' came the response, as he did his fly up.

'Well, do it somewhere else!' I shot back. 'Not in my front garden!'

The lad got back in the car then, shouting obscenities in my general direction, while another of them rolled the window down and yelled something about coming back with a gun.

Which Paul, who'd been hovering up on the landing all this time, heard. So, even as I was shutting the front door, unconcerned - to me, they'd they just looked like a bunch of rowdy teenagers – he was rattling down the stairs, panicking, insisting we put every light out in the house and that we must go and hide under the dining room table. The next thing I knew, as the lights went off all around me, was that he was making a 999 call and getting the police round.

But he wasn't wholly overreacting, because no sooner had the house been plunged into total darkness than the car was back, the boys having decided there was fun to be had; they were now out of their car and yelling at me to come out and face them.

Paul was terrified now, but I wasn't scared of a bunch of idiot boys. I'd been brought up in circumstances that had toughened me up, and I had no intention of being intimidated in my own home. Crucially, I had two dogs, one of which was a German Shepherd – if I couldn't send them packing, I didn't doubt they'd be able to.

'Go on!' I said to them both, opening the front door and letting them out of it, 'go get 'em!' Dawn and Spring duly ran up the driveway, barking and growling and, as I'd suspected would happen, the lads were back in the car and speeding off up the lane before you could say 'Alsatian'.

The police arrived two minutes later. We invited them in, and they were lovely, and there was a degree of amusement as they noted the details, but Paul was furious, ranting on about how I could easily have been shot. And the look in his eye should have warned me.

The very moment they left he rounded on me, eyes flashing, his lip curled in fury. 'You're an idiot!' he raged. 'You could have put both our lives in jeopardy!'

I tried to reason with him. I pointed out that they were just young and silly, that no harm had been done, that the dogs had seen them off in a moment. But the more I tried to calm him down, the nastier he became. It was as if nothing I could say on the entire spectrum from 'don't overreact' to 'I'm sorry' would halt the escalation of his fury.

Was he just reacting to his earlier fear, or looking for an outlet for his earlier anger? Either way, I became aware of Dawn, now stationed in front of me, leaning in to my legs in an obvious protective gesture.

Which Paul obviously didn't see, because he went for me then, lunging forwards to grab my T-Shirt, causing Dawn to spring forwards between us and start barking.

Paul stopped then, momentarily, shocked and uncertain, but even so took one small further step. It was enough. Dawn lunged at him, full force, rearing up on two legs, knocking him effortlessly to the ground. She then stood astride him, growling softly, her nose almost touching his.

'Call her off,' Paul whispered.

I did so immediately. But she stayed where she was. It took a second attempt to have her reluctantly release him and return to her place at my side.

'That dog is dangerous,' Paul said quietly, as he scrambled back up to his feet, his gaze not leaving Dawn for an instant.

'No, she's just protective of me,' I corrected. There seemed nothing else to say. She'd proved it amply, after all. And perhaps that would spell an end to – or at least a reduction in – Paul's fiery temper. I hoped so. Either way, as he carefully skirted round the pair of us and went back to bed, the stupid teenage boys were forgotten.

As spring became summer, and our fledgling business began taking shape, things became a little less volatile between us, and I felt much happier. I wasn't sure if it was Dawn's constant protective presence by my side or just a drop in both our stress levels generally, but while we still rowed – I could still seem to wind Paul up by uttering even the most unlikely thing – there was no repeat of the aggression I'd seen that night.

And when Paul wasn't wound up, he was a pleasure to be around. He was doing something he loved and clearly had a huge talent for; working long hours to create the tools and equipment we'd need. And the work not only gave him pleasure; it also meant we were living less in each other's pockets than we might have been, which helped a lot.

Money, however, was still a big issue. By now, Roger was paying dribs and drabs of what he owed us, but things were still extremely precarious financially - a situation we knew wouldn't change until everything had been built or purchased and we had our first scheduled event in October, which was still a few months away.

'I know,' said Paul one day, while we were pondering our dwindling bank balance. 'You know what we should do? We should get more chickens!'

It would be a glimpse into Paul's psyche that I would have done well to heed.

By this time we were something of a menagerie in the making. We had six cats, two dogs, two young goats (who caused havoc) and were also realising that the livery business we'd inherited wasn't the 'money for old rope' sideline we'd anticipated. As a couple of townies, we knew nothing about stabling horses and ponies and it was already proving to be something of a chore. The animals were lovely, but the owners were demanding, to say the least. Our grass was always wrong - either too long or too short, our hay either too green or too brown. There weren't enough fences, or there were too many fences, and the owners would think nothing of turning up at silly o'clock in the morning or late in the evening to point our inadequacies out.

The chickens, in contrast, didn't come with exacting owners, as we'd bought half a dozen of them ourselves, back in the spring, from a local man called Rob. They were a breed called Black Rock and, with the hen houses already there, were an obvious addition – having them around meant we'd always have eggs.

Collecting our first home-laid ones had been a real thrill as well, so even though it seemed unnecessary, I didn't bat too much of an eyelid when Paul returned from seeing Rob – with whom we'd immediately struck up an easy friendship – with half a dozen more only a week later.

But twelve were surely enough. We already had more eggs than we could eat.

'More?' I asked him, shocked.

'Yes,' he said. 'I was thinking of around a hundred.'

Now I was open-mouthed. 'A *hundred* hens? Why on earth would we want to do that?'

'As a *business*,' he said, rolling his eyes, as if I was some kind of idiot for not immediately sharing his vision.

'As in selling the eggs?'

'Of course as in selling the eggs!'

'But supposing we can't find anyone to buy them?'

'Of course we'll find people to buy them! Everyone's getting into organic and free-range these days!'

And so it went on, in the now familiar way, with my raising reasonable questions and objections and Paul accusing me of being negative - dismissing each of my questions irritably and with an increasingly raised voice, and eventually shouting at me in the same way he always did – for putting a dampener on every single idea he ever had.

So I caved in. When his mind was made up there was no deflecting him anyway. He'd do it whether I agreed with it or not.

He duly did, setting about preparing for their arrival with gusto, getting all the chicken houses ready and erecting a huge fence around the chicken run, to stop any foxes getting in and killing them. It was a major undertaking and represented another dent in our fragile finances, but as it was a new business initiative Paul was adamant it was worth doing things properly.

The chickens duly arrived – not the hundred he'd told me, but *two* hundred of them, all squashed in horrifically tiny cages on a giant truck. It was upsetting to see, and even more so when we got them all installed in their hen houses to see them huddling together in one corner, seemingly too terrified to move, having been used to such inhumane confinement since birth.

It didn't take long, however, for them to acclimatise and start exploring their new environment, and within a couple of weeks they were happily wandering around outside with the bemused goats.

There was also the small matter of the eggs. Unsurprisingly, we were now getting a lot of them, and, since selling them was the whole reason for having two hundred chickens in the first place, selling them was what we had to get on and do. Paul's master plan for achieving this (and he really hadn't thought beyond it) was to make a sign and put it up outside the house. And, despite the fact that we were so isolated the lane hardly ever saw any traffic, a couple of people did stop and buy a box or two. But it was a drop in the ocean compared to what our enthusiastic hens were producing. The only other regular outlet we had was Paul's father. With Paul's parents quite regular visitors, he provided a useful conduit, always taking several dozen to try and sell at work. We'd also give dozens away to friends for free, which we were happy to do, but, given the cost of feed and the labour involved, we needed to start trying to break even, at least, even if the idea of making a profit now felt like an impossible dream.

The eggs just kept coming. And that drop in the ocean was beginning to feel more and more microscopic. We desperately needed to find a way to sell on a much larger scale. 'So we'll start an egg round,' Paul announced one morning in May, as if he'd single-handedly come up with Nuclear Fission.

'An egg round?' I asked, wondering what sort of thing he had in mind. Did he imagine we'd don jaunty outfits and trot round the streets with wicker baskets in the crook of our arms?

Almost. 'We'll drive around,' he explained, 'and sell door to door. And see if we can set up some regular orders.'

I was filled with gloom; I was up for most things but the thought of becoming some sort of rural door-to-door salesman appalled me. Paul, however, couldn't wait to get started, and soon had the car filled with eggs. Having no other kind of plan, I had no choice but to go with him and give it a try – at least I couldn't then be accused of being negative.

We drove to a local densely populated area and at the start of a busy looking street Paul pulled in. 'Go on,' he said, 'go and knock at that house over there and ask them if they'd like to buy any eggs.'

'Why me?' I thought, but didn't say. Paul was driving and I knew he'd have the answer straight away – I could do the asking a bit more easily than he could. He could just drive alongside me, carrying the stock.

I walked up to the front door and knocked, but there was thankfully no answer. 'Try next door!' Paul enthused from the car.

This time I got 'lucky'. A woman opened the door to me.

'We're selling local free range eggs,' I explained. 'Would you like to buy some?'

She looked at me suspiciously, then out to where Paul was sitting in our old VW Scirocco. It perhaps wouldn't have been so bad if we'd at least had a van with a picture of some chickens on the side. As it was, I imagine we both just looked, well, dodgy. This wasn't 1940's wartime Britain, after all.

I could see her point. Would I buy half a dozen eggs off a pair of drive-by strangers on my doorstep? I very much doubted it.

Nor would she, it seemed. 'No thank you,' she said, politely, and shut the door.

'*You* do it,' I huffed, as I got back into the car. And, perhaps reading the signs, Paul duly did. It took several goes and several houses before he managed to sell half a dozen, but, buoyed by this tiny victory, he then went into overdrive and within a couple of hours we'd sold six dozen eggs between us. Perhaps, if I could just quash my queasiness about the whole door-to-door thing, here *was* a way we could make the chickens pay.

I duly buttoned my lip and tried to throw myself into it with the same enthusiasm Paul had, and after much early legwork we got into a routine of doing three days of rounds every week, returning to the three different areas we'd initially pitched.

Paul had the details of every client meticulously recorded, as well, as was his precise way. Not just their address and what they'd ordered, but a 'profile' of each, including everything he felt might be of use to us for future ordering - right down to hair colour and what sort of personality they seemed to have.

At the time this attention to detail never stuck me as odd. Paul had an HND in business studies, as he reminded me often, and I assumed that this kind of in-depth client profiling was just a part of what he'd been taught about how to make a business succeed.

We were a long way from that – we still weren't bringing in enough to pay for the chicken feed, let alone the rest of us. And by this time that was no small outlay either, because though we'd tragically lost three of our cats to speeding motorists, we'd managed to acquire two further dogs. One was a Jack Russell bitch, BJ, that Paul had brought home from the chicken man one day (his mum bred them), and the other was a huge elderly collie who just turned up at the house one day in a terrible state, starving and exhausted.

We took him down to the Dogs Trust in the hopes that there would be a family somewhere who were missing him, but it seemed not. With him being so elderly and in such a bad way, I felt terrible at the thought of him spending his last years stuck in a cage. So we took him in as well, despite him being another mouth to feed.

All of which meant that every penny we could earn really counted. And at least with the egg run we weren't losing as much as we could have been. So with Paul keen to continue, I stopped putting objections in his way. Perhaps at some point he'd find a way to get us into the black.

But this was always supposed to be a sideline; we were in the middle of setting up the games business. And we were now toiling in earnest, with Paul completing the casino tables while I tried to drum up new bookings. And succeeding, too. By the time our first event came around – three casino tables for a hotel in the Cotswolds - it finally felt like we were at last running something with potential.

There was just the small matter of the two hundred chickens. Now that our time was almost fully occupied, and we could no longer make a dent in the egg mountain with deliveries, it seemed to be growing exponentially.

'They'll have to go,' Paul decided one day, out of the blue. I didn't argue. In fact, inwardly, I cheered. He duly placed an ad in the local paper, the flame of enthusiasm for the project being snuffed out as instantaneously as had the rush of enthusiasm that had begun it. Over the next few weeks, little by little, they began being taken off our hands, then, having forgotten to close the houses one night before going off to do an event, we returned to find a fox had finished off the last thirty or so.

It was heartbreaking clearing the bodies away, but it was also a watershed; the egg delivery business was well and truly over, and, bit by bit, the egg mountain disappeared as well.

In its place, however, something else had begun piling up; evidence of Paul's growing eccentricities.

The only problem was that I didn't see them.

CHAPTER NINE

ONE BORN
EVERY MINUTE

With the chickens gone, the need for chicken feed had at least gone as well, but the fledgling games business was still leaching money. It had become so tight, in fact, that I was constantly on the look out for ways to get hold of some just to manage the weekly food shop. It was therefore a no brainer when I was approached outside Tesco one afternoon in March 1988 and asked if I'd be interested in going to a timeshare presentation locally; the carrot was £25 worth of M&S vouchers.

It was the usual hard-sell approach but I accepted that. Selling timeshares in holiday homes was big business at that time, and everyone knew how it worked. You had to go as a couple and you had to sit through an intense two-hour presentation, but I could cope with wasting two hours of my life if there was going to be £25 at the end of it.

Paul agreed – I'd made the appointment for a Sunday, as I knew he'd never agree otherwise – and we duly turned up at the allotted hour the following weekend. The place was a stately home called Walton Hall and was suitably impressive. Once owned by the king of drag queens, the legendary Danny la Rue, it had a fabulous entrance hall and ballroom, and the rest of the building, including the old stables had been converted into luxury apartments.

The hard sell to get us signed up began in earnest. We were paired up with a guy called Martin, a Londoner, which meant I related to him immediately, though as he started his spiel I almost immediately zoned out from what he was telling us, having heard it all before.

Paul had not. In fact, as the selling continued I could see he was becoming more and more attentive, and beginning to ask lots of probing questions. And when we did the tour and watched the obligatory sales video, I could sense he was getting genuinely excited about the prospect, which worried me – was this going to be Chicken Run all over again?

'Yes,' he said firmly, when the sales pitch was finally over and Martin popped the inevitable 'did we want to buy one?' question.

I groaned inwardly. This wasn't the plan. 'But we don't even take holidays!' I argued.

'Exactly!' Paul retorted, his enthusiasm coming off him like an aura. 'And we should. And if we buy one, it'll *make* us take holidays. It'll be an incentive to – don't you see?'

I caught Martin's eye and felt a familiar heartsink moment. I'd been in and around sales for years and I could read his expression. He must have thought we'd been parachuted in from heaven. It must have been the easiest sell he'd ever made; something I would come to find out was known as 'a walkover'.

There was no counter-argument I could offer that would make Paul change his mind, and we celebrated that night with champagne that had been gifted to us by the company. Champagne that was probably a drop in the proverbial ocean compared to their commission. And, as ever, Paul was thrilled by his shrewd business acumen, patting himself on the back for having made such a great investment.

I wasn't convinced. If it was that good why did they have to sell it so aggressively? But Paul was having none of it. He felt that not only were the holidays exceptional value, the whole package was in itself highly saleable, so that, should we decide to sell at any point, we'd make a profit on that as well. He was so chuffed, in fact, that he announced the next day that he wanted to go back and buy another week.

I was aghast. And I tried every counter argument, as was becoming the norm now, but he just regurgitated the same sales talk we'd been given by Martin the previous day and in the end managed to convince me, if not of the enormous value in the product, at least of the fact that he was not going to be swayed. We went back that evening and when Paul said we'd like to purchase a second week, Martin almost fell of his chair.

Looking back, I wonder still at my capitulation. But then, hindsight is a wonderful thing. At the time I still believed that Paul *did* have business acumen; he was a natural entrepreneur, or so I saw it - a man not only with charisma, but also enormous energy and passion. When he believed in something he went for it, giving it his all, and putting in incredibly long hours; it was one of the qualities, however dark the dark parts of his psyche were, that I perhaps admired in him most.

So I got on with the business of keeping positive and optimistic, pushing my natural caution about the financial commitment to the furthest reaches of my mind, and believing that once the games business really took off, the financial pressure - and the stress it created - would ease.

And there was one immediate positive I could take advantage of. Buying the timeshares gave us free membership of the leisure club at Walton Hall, which included a small gym that nobody ever seemed to go in and a lavish and similarly empty swimming pool. It suited me perfectly, and I started going swimming and training in the gym there several times a week. Most importantly, I went there alone. With Paul and I living and working together 24/7 I desperately needed some time on my own. We both did – even with the healthiest relationship in the world, people need time apart to do their own thing. So it was good for us, and good in an unexpected way too.

One afternoon, after I'd been for a swim and was in the bar buying a juice, I was approached by the manager, who I'd by now got to know, along the several of the staff. He asked how the new business was going and when I told him it was still a bit slow, he suggested I should try selling timeshares myself. 'You'd be good at it,' he assured me, 'and it would be a nice bit of extra income.'

I couldn't see it myself, but he explained that, actually, most people who sold it were owners themselves, just like me – the people who could really see the benefits.

Again, I wasn't sure – I'd yet to see any benefits - but, when I got home, Paul agreed that I should, too. And though it didn't really feel 'me' there was another important upside. It would give us even more time apart from each other, something which was beginning to feel less like a privilege and more like an essential.

I duly agreed to start a training course, and right away, it was as if a weight had been lifted from me. Everything about our always-volatile relationship felt easier in smaller doses, even those times (and they were increasing in frequency) when Paul's obsession with his ideas and enthusiasm for pursuing them bordered on the febrile.

And once we had our new routine in place, or lives began changing in lots of little ways. Though they were about to change more radically than I thought.

By the time I started selling timeshares we had more or less settled into our new rural environment. We'd made a few friends – including the chicken man, and a few scattered neighbours – and most evenings now Paul would finish the working day by heading to the pub with some of them for a spot of 'early doors' drinking. Which was fine, but as with anything that Paul became enthused by, it was all or nothing. He'd go for months without drinking when on some health kick or other - but when he got back on it, he got back on it good and proper. So by the time I'd agreed to selling timeshares, a new domestic routine had already arisen – one in which I'd cook dinner for us both only to throw it away hours later, when he came home roaring drunk in the small hours.

Now I had my new job, I would often work long into the evenings, which meant I wasn't home to cook a meal for us anyway. Now, instead of going home, I'd often just head straight to the pub as well; a case of 'if you can't beat them, join them'. I certainly had no appetite for going home and cooking for me alone.

We carried on in this way for a couple of months, with my heart not really in it when it came to the aggressive selling, and my financial fortunes varying every bit as much as I'd anticipated. I could get home after a weekend's work thinking I'd made a thousand pounds in commission, then, by the end of Monday, watch as it dwindled to almost nothing, as buyer after buyer, having got home and thought it through properly, called – as they had a right to – to cancel. 'Walkovers' like Paul and I were clearly thin on the ground.

As was any clear thinking on my part, as to where our relationship was going, since we were both, in our own way, avoiding addressing it, every bit as much as we were avoiding going home and eating a civilised evening meal together.

That was to change on an evening in June 1989, when I decided to have a clear out of the freezer. I'd found some burgers in the bottom of it which I knew we'd never use so, to save wasting them, I decided to cook them off for the dogs.

They all dived in appreciatively and I thought no more about it, until later on that evening when I noticed Dawn had become listless, and was just laying lethargically in the middle of the kitchen floor. I left her there to rest, thinking that perhaps she'd just had an energetic day, but then she started vomiting as well. She was clearly quite unwell, too, because once she'd started she couldn't seem to stop being sick either, and, worryingly, what was coming up was getting darker and darker.

I called the vet and explained her symptoms and he told me not to worry. Just to keep her warm and calm and bring her in the following morning. And I was reassured when I managed to coax her upstairs to the bedroom, as usual, so she could sleep on the floor beside the bed.

Again, she settled, but I was to be lulled into a false sense of security. When I woke up in the morning, she was no longer by my side. She'd made it as far as the bedroom door, and died where she lay.

I was devastated, heartbroken, torn up with guilt. Would things have been different if I'd only taken her to the vet the previous night? I was in too much of a state to ring our own vet and trust myself not to become hysterical, so instead I rang the local Dogs Trust and asked them which vet they used, and called them instead Had it been the burgers? Was it some underlying problem? I was desperate to know what had killed her. She was such a young dog, but with her history of being starved had they been too much for her?

They were incredibly kind to me, telling me that if I took her body down to them, they would try and ascertain what they could. And they did; telling me that her pancreas had started digesting itself - that was why she was vomiting blood – and that there would have been nothing anyone could have done to save her.

I felt even worse; she must have died in agony, but, being the kind of dog she was, she wouldn't have wanted to make a fuss and wake me – so typical of her. They tried to reassure me; saying it could have happened at any time; that the burgers weren't necessarily the trigger, but it was hard not to blame myself. It still is. I still miss her today, all those years later.

The loss of my beloved Dawn was not only devastating, it was life-changing too, because Paul's behaviour towards me altered almost overnight. I knew he had always been wary of her since the night she'd made it clear she'd protect me from him, whatever it took, but I don't think I'd fully taken on board just *how* terrified he'd been of her. But he must have been, because the change in him after her death was as swift as it was dramatic.

His aggression – something that had been so tempered for so long that I'd begun to take the new, milder Paul for granted – seemed to return with a vengeance. Gone were logical discussions, gone too were the days when he would only touch me with affection – we were back to blistering arguments and physical abuse.

I was also reminded what a warped relationship he had with his parents; something that I was able to witness in chilling detail. They were staying with us for the weekend, just a few weeks after Dawn's death, when some argument – I have no idea what about, but something trivial certainly – sparked Paul's reliably unpredictable temper. His anger was directed at all three of us on this occasion and I could see it was escalating quickly. I tried to calm him down but this was a trigger to an escalation of his anger in itself and, to his parent's horror, he suddenly grabbed me by the throat, slamming me against the living room wall while I screamed at him to stop.

His parents seemed paralysed; they just stood and gaped, unwilling and unable to intervene, and though the other dogs – Spring, Hobo and BJ – were all barking at him, they weren't Dawn and didn't intervene either.

Paul let me go moments later of his own volition, but it was only to throw things instead. He was no less angry – if anything he seemed even more furious, and as his father finally started trying to reason with him, and his mother become hysterical (both of which seemed to inflame him even further), he started picking up whatever he could lay hands on to chuck at me. First came a mug, then the TV remote, then an assortment of cushions and chairs. He kicked the settee repeatedly till it was beached on its back, all the while dodging both his father and my attempts to restrain him.

But there was worse to come. Still shouting and raging, but finding himself all out of missiles, his gaze came to rest on the coffee table. I felt overcome with dread, following his gaze, knowing how heavy it was and what he was about to do with it, too. And he did. In a terrifying re-enactment of the scene in his chalet at Butlins, he picked it up and hurled it not at me, as I'd expected, but straight at one of the patio doors.

He threw it with such force that it went straight through and into the garden, smashing the glass into a million pieces.

'What the fuck do you think you're doing?!' I shouted, aghast at what he'd done. 'Look!' I said. 'Look!! Are you insane?!'

There was no response. Breathing heavily, he just stormed out of the living room, his mother, sobbing and gulping, chasing after him.

Paul's father was silent for a moment, and than he found his voice. 'What's wrong with him?' he asked. 'What's wrong with him, Vikie?' he kept on saying it, too, again and again.

We both heard the sound of Paul's car roaring off and then his mother returned moments later. She was crying still, no less hysterically than she had been since the start, casting her eyes about at the scene of devastation in our living room and through huge racking sobs asking me what had turned her beautiful son into this person she didn't know.

'He needs help!' she kept saying to me. 'He's under much too much pressure! He's clearly not coping! He needs help!'

I couldn't have agreed more, but I knew exactly what she was implying; that there'd been nothing wrong with him till he met me and that I'd somehow managed to damage him: never – not *ever* – that he might be mentally ill. And I knew that if I so much as hinted that he might be, there was a real chance that it wouldn't be the patio door that a piece of heavy furniture was directed at next.

So there was nothing to be discussed and the aftermath of all the violence was depressingly predictable. He'd behaved like a monster – like a giant toddler throwing his toys out of the pram – but as a thirty-three year old man, without the least concern about the damage he might have inflicted and, as ever, it was the world, not Paul, that was deemed at fault.

And it seemed it always would be. Though when we were alone later, his father expressed concern at how violently Paul had treated me, the following day it was as if nothing had happened. While Paul had been absent, his father had gone and found some plywood to cover the open doorway, and the next day, when Paul asked him if he'd come with him to buy some glass, they both calmly trotted off as if the whole thing was just another DIY job. No mention of what had caused the incident was ever made again.

And perhaps it had been the break in this behaviour when Dawn was alive that now flagged it up for me now so forcibly; this was the *real* Paul. The one who would not be crossed, *ever*. The one with the terrifying temper. The one, moreover, who could lose it so comprehensively that he would hurl tables through plate glass windows – and without, it seemed, so much as a shred of remorse. What was I doing staying with such a man? Was I insane?

It was the wake up call I needed and I heeded it. And now I had my job, I began thinking about how I could extricate myself from his clutches and make a new life for myself – one away from his aggression and domination. I even plucked up the courage to book a fortnight in Spain on my own, just to get some distance between us and have space to think. He was livid, but once I found the courage to defy him, I realised I was stronger than I thought.

'I need to get away,' I told him. 'Because I don't know where our relationship is going and I need space to think what to do.'

Paul totally disagreed with me, just as I'd known he would, but I stood my ground and I went, and when I returned, having experienced the calm of not being pushed around and shouted at, I told him in no uncertain terms that it was over.

He was aghast. Shocked to the core at the conclusion I'd reached. 'But we are *made* for each other!' he asserted. 'How can you want to throw away such a perfect relationship?'

Perhaps that was what clinched it; that this hell was his idea of 'perfect'. Even with my past, and the toxic relationships I'd grown up with and been in, I still knew that perfect this wasn't.

My decision made, and Paul finally accepting that I meant it, we began to make plans to unravel our joint lives. He would re-mortgage the house and continue to run our casino business, while I, once I had my half share of the equity, would move back to London and start afresh. We'd not had sex for five months by now, and our relationship was truly over, and once Paul digested that fact, I felt he had begun to understand that too, and began to be nice to me for the first time in years.

It was perhaps the worst thing that could have happened. We were still working together, attending events, because we had no choice but to do so, and it was after one such, in Hereford, that my plans became unravelled: with the pressure off in every sense, and our separation imminent, we ended up sleeping together.

I couldn't believe it was happening, but at the same time, I didn't want to stop it. It was the first time I'd received any physical affection from him - from another human being - in such a long time. I had no one else, after all. I had no loving family, no close, meaningful friendships, no support network, no bolt-hole, no one to scream 'no, Vikie, don't!' and drag me away.

It was as if our lives were just too tangled up together. We'd been alone together for so long now, both emotionally and geographically, that perhaps I'd lost the power of rational thought. I have no idea what possessed me to let my barrier down that night. All I know is that to feel wanted by Paul again - to have him desire me and to cherish me - was almost like a drug.

But I would go on to pay for my moment of insanity. Two months later, unbelievably, I discovered I was pregnant - and Paul wanted a family more than anything in the world.

CHAPTER TEN
DESTINY'S CHILD

I was lost, totally lost. And so alone.

I had no one to talk to, and that was perhaps the biggest single problem. No loving mum to share my news with, no clear-sighted sisters, no friend with whom I could sit down and talk myself hoarse about the most unexpected and potentially life-changing thing to have yet happened in my life.

Had I had any sort of support, from people who cared passionately for my welfare, things might have been very different. As it was, I had no real family any more. Though my eldest brother lived in Coventry, our relationship had always been fraught and given what had happened between us when I was a child, we would never be close. My other brother, Tony, was at that time still living with my father, but, though we saw them both three or four times a year, his autism meant such relationship as we had was one of polite conversation and nothing more.

I should have hung on to my old friends. That's what came back to me time and time again. Though it would only be hindsight that taught me how much I'd been manipulated, I found myself in a place of complete isolation, as, one by one, under Paul's influence and his need to be completely insular, I'd let them all slip away.

Still, I wonder if it would have made any difference anyway. The sad truth was that even had I anyone close enough to talk to about it, I probably wouldn't have done so, for fear he'd find out.

As it was, I didn't have the luxury in any case; there was no network of longstanding close friends to call on when I needed them; my strange childhood and fractured education had seen to that. Yes, I had lots of 'friends' of the acquaintance variety, but we'd spent so long building our business, working with just one another, in isolation, that I didn't even have a group of work colleagues to call my own. I had no one, bar Paul. And I was terrified.

My pregnancy crept up on me unawares. Despite what had passed between Paul and I at the work event, and his tentative suggestions immediately afterwards that we should have a re-think about splitting up, I was still determined to leave him, and told him so. It had been a one-off, a mistake made under the influence of alcohol, and, for both our sakes, we must part company as planned.

But as the days passed, I began feeling more and more sluggish; ill in a way I couldn't put my finger on. So, wanting to feel strong again, in readiness for dismantling our lives together and starting afresh, I made an appointment with the local GP.

In my entire life, I'd never had more than two or three periods a year, and as the gap between them could sometimes stretch to as much as six or seven months, when the GP asked me the date of my last period and I told him, pregnancy couldn't have been further from either of our minds. My history of polycystic ovaries and almost certain infertility was right there in my medical records, after all. I even had the dubious distinction of having had that confirmed again during my twenties by no less that Mr Pinker, The Queen's Gynaecologist. He'd also told me that it was unlikely that medical technology would advance sufficiently in my reproductive lifetime for there to be any chance of my ever having children.

And that had been okay by me, because I had never wanted any. I had never been maternal, due to the traumas of my own childhood. I'd never been around babies either. Children simply weren't on my radar – I wasn't even an auntie – and the idea of being a mother wasn't remotely in my mental universe. Right now, I was more concerned that I was feeling so poorly, and what might be done to address it.

My GP thought it was probably due to my hormones. He prescribed some pills that would induce a period in the hopes that having one would settle them down.

'You mustn't take them,' Paul said when I returned from the doctor's surgery, having collected my prescription on the way home.

'Why ever not?' I asked him, already irritated that he should even think it was any of his business any more.

'Because you might be pregnant!' he said.

I think I laughed out loud. It was such a ridiculous notion, after all.

Had Paul's parents not been at the house when I returned from the doctor's perhaps – just perhaps – I would have taken those pills; gobbled them up and put and end to that kind of speculation once and for all. But as soon as the idea was out there (and I perhaps should have realised Paul would leap upon it as a possibility) it was as if taking the pills would be tantamount to murder.

In the end, fed up with being interrogated by both Paul and his mother, I took myself off to bed, still feeling sick to the stomach. By the time I came back down, still feeling nauseous, he'd flushed the pills down the loo, and had also come up with an idea.

'You're not well,' he said. '*Clearly*. So rather than take pills, I think you need to go back to the GP and ask to be referred to a specialist.'

I agreed. I *was* ll. I felt terrible, in fact. So, with my thoughts firmly fixed on the possibility of feeling better, I agreed. But when the appointment came through it was for a date four months in the future; a long time to be waking up every morning feeling such a powerful need to either throw up or stay in bed.

'We'll have to go private,' Paul insisted, which, again, was out of character, but since the night we'd slept together he'd been much softer towards me; solicitous, appreciative, keeping a rein on his temper, acting as if he really cared for my wellbeing. It had made no difference to my plans; I was much too familiar with these cycles, but right now I felt vulnerable and sick to my stomach, so I was happy to take advantage of this gesture of kindness, even though we couldn't really afford it.

The new appointment came through, for a date three weeks hence, though as we had an event that day in Bournemouth, Paul couldn't go with me; he'd drive down in the van to get set up and I'd join him later. And so it was that on a dreary Wednesday in October 1990, I went to meet a consultant gynaecologist called Mr Hughes, who would go on to become an incredibly important part of my life for the next eleven years.

Mr Hughes asked me about my symptoms and history and I told him everything. Having already seen my notes, he agreed that it was probably impossible that I was pregnant but as he examined me he told me that my uterus was enlarged to the point it would be if I was - by approximately eight weeks.

I laughed but, on a serious note, asked him what else could cause the swelling. He told me that there were a number of more sinister possibilities but that we would rule out pregnancy first, because that was obviously standard clinical practice. He then booked me in for scan on the Friday and told me to bring a urine sample to the hospital the next day.

I drove on down to Bournemouth thinking dark thoughts. With the idea of pregnancy ruled out already as far as I was concerned, I wondered what exactly this mysterious swelling might be. I'd never worried about my health – I was the polar opposite of a hypochondriac – but as I drove, I kept trying to work out if I felt different in my uterus. Was there a growth there perhaps? A tumour? Something that was indeed sinister? How could it not be, if I was feeling like this?

I took the sample in the next day and tried not to worry, convincing myself that as I'd had lots of cysts over the years this was just another one of those. And I did a good job of talking myself out of my anxiety, because when the timing of the scan clashed with an appointment with our accountant, Bill, I left he and Paul discussing accounts and tax returns in his office, fully expecting to be back in a couple of hours, with nothing changed and the weight of anxiety off my mind, even if the feeling of malaise still remained.

I had never set foot in an antenatal clinic before, and was disorientated to find myself in one now; I was surrounded by expectant mothers with huge bumps, and my only thought was how little I'd want to become one myself. I had zero maternal instinct and with the split from Paul coming together finally I was actually feeling as though I was gaining control of my life again, and pregnancy, to my mind, was the antithesis of that.

So it was with nothing more than a bemused sense of being in a slightly alien environment that I went into the room where the radiographer was waiting, took off my skirt, as instructed, and lay down on the bed. It was to be a feeling that would be extremely short-lived.

'There!' she said, after what felt like ages of having the paddle moved over my stomach. She turned her computer screen around so I could see what she was seeing too. 'There you go,' she repeated cheerfully, as I sat up to look. 'You can see the heartbeat!'

I think my brain registered the word 'heartbeat' a couple of seconds after my eyes did and as soon as that happened I flopped back against the pillow, stunned and trying desperately to take it in. This wasn't happening. It couldn't be. I couldn't possibly be pregnant.

'Congratulations!' the radiographer said, obviously expecting me to be delighted. And clearly oblivious to the fact that I wasn't. Little did she know.

The pregnancy confirmed, I was then called straight in to see Mr Hughes and by the time I walked into his office, tears were streaming down my face. I hoped against hope that I'd imagined it, prayed that it was all a big mistake, but, no, my baby would apparently be born in early May the following year.

Which left me no choice but to ask the question that had formed in my head if not my lips when I'd heard the word 'heartbeat'. Would it be possible to terminate the pregnancy?

'Yes, it would,' he confirmed. 'Because you're only eight weeks pregnant. But I suggest you speak to the baby's father and discuss all your options before making such a huge decision.'

And he was right. I knew I had to tell Paul. Despite everything, I knew I had no right to keep something like this from him, even if deep down, I had a strong conviction that I should ultimately be the one to decide what to do. But 'discuss'? There would be no discussion here. I already knew Paul would be over the moon, not least because he'd always wanted children desperately, and was already behaving like an over-excited puppy at the possibility, however many times I'd told him it couldn't be. It was also a breakthrough in terms of our own future; I knew he'd see it as a way of keeping us together.

Heart in mouth, my mind teeming with options and questions, I rang him at Bill's office from the payphone at the hospital, and all I could hear were his shouts and screams of joy as he leapt around, the excitement in his voice palpable.

I couldn't have felt more desperate. What sort of joke was Mother Nature playing with me now? I still have no words that describe just how wretched and despairing I felt that day. I knew in my heart that staying with Paul would eventually destroy me but at the same time the one thing I couldn't begin to countenance would be to try and bring this baby up on my own, for all the reasons that meant I had no one to turn to about the pregnancy. I had no money, no partner, no family, no friends, and I'd never wanted a baby in the first place. How would I love it and care for it and bring it up all alone? I didn't even know how to hold a baby properly, and, worse, I recoiled at the very thought.

I returned to Bill's office to meet Paul on leaden feet, desperately trying to hold myself together, but falling apart increment by devastating increment, as the reality of my situation sank in. Perhaps, had I been irresponsible about contraception, I might have felt differently, but I had been *told* I was infertile. How could fate be so cruel?

When I arrived, the whole of Bill's office erupted in congratulation; a sea of smiling faces and a flurry of applause and, in the middle of it was Paul, jumping up and down like a lunatic, beaming and whooping with joy. He picked me up and span me round, dancing me round and round the office – too fast for anyone to properly make out the traumatised and bewildered expression on my face.

I felt devastated at the prospect of ending a life, but an abortion seemed only one workable solution. How could I bring a child into such a mess of a relationship? Which I knew would still be a mess even if I tried to go it alone. It wasn't like Paul would disappear in a puff of smoke, was it? He'd be part of my life, then, for as long as I lived. No, there was no other choice. Staying with Paul was unthinkable and bringing a child up alone was unthinkable so, in the end, after days and nights of wretched indecision, I secretly pulled out the yellow pages one afternoon and found a clinic in Birmingham where the deed could be done.

In truth, I wished then that I'd never told Paul. It might have been the moral choice but now it felt like the wrong one. As it was, I knew I'd have to be extremely careful from here on in – make up some story, get the pregnancy terminated and then simply tell him I'd miscarried. But it wasn't to be as simple as that because when I went for my appointment I was told I would then need to return for a second, to give me time to think it through; after all, they explained, I might change my mind.

In reality, I'd never been surer of anything, however distressing it was to think about what I was about to do. But feeling so alone in the world, paradoxically, made me stronger. Better to never know the infant I was carrying; that way I wouldn't have to cope with the hurt of seeing him or her every day, knowing their conception should never have happened, and they would never have the life they deserved. If I knew anything, that much I did know. I never wanted a child of mine to have to live through a childhood like my own. The second appointment couldn't come around quick enough.

I might have been a 'good working model' in my day but I was obviously no good as an actress, and, as a result, my termination was scuppered before it even began. But perhaps, given our circumstances, it wouldn't have taken a rocket scientist to work out what I was planning and, leaving nothing to chance, Paul had followed me to my second pre-termination appointment. He confronted me about it as soon as I got home, and then began one unholy and protracted row.

He started off from a position of moral superiority, accusing me of almost every crime imaginable. How dare I sneak off and try to abort his baby? He had a right to have a say in the future of his baby and I had violated that right in trying to kill it.

I kept trying to state my case; that we were splitting up, that our relationship was completely untenable; that I didn't want a baby – that I couldn't *cope* with having a baby. That every fibre of my being knew this was wrong on every level, that we shouldn't be bringing a child into the world that we were not going to be able to give a decent life.

'Then *I'll* bring it up!' he yelled. 'And my mum and dad will help me! *I* want this baby, even if you don't, Vikie, so you have *no* right to abort it and I'm not going to let you!'

He became physical then, pushing and shoving me around the kitchen - always his first expression of violence towards me. And as I tried to fight back with words, repeating that I was *not* going to bring a life into the world in these circumstances however much he shouted, he eventually started punching me in the kidneys to reinforce his words, knowing that, at some point, I would give in. And with no energy to fight him, and nowhere to go, I gave up trying to fight back and let him. And even as I wondered when he'd stop hitting me, the irony didn't escape me: perhaps he'd cause me to lose the baby in any case.

Chapter Eleven
THE IRON LADY

The child I had never believed I'd be able to have was born in the early hours of 19th of May, 1991. I was 33 years old and had believed myself infertile, yet by some twist of fate (I remember thinking ruefully that only time would tell if it was a cruel twist) I had just given birth. It had been a harrowing labour that marked the end of a harrowing pregnancy, and the moment my baby was plonked unceremoniously on my chest I was completely overwhelmed. It was not, however, by joy or a rush of maternal love. I was just overwhelmed by this enormous sense of responsibility. This was my child? Apparently so. Someone told me it was a girl. And I clearly remember thinking 'oh, I have a daughter'. But the red thing that was currently writhing on my chest didn't feel as if it had anything to do with me.

I had at least reached a place of acceptance by this time, a process that had begun fourteen weeks into the pregnancy. Once I had agreed that I was going to have the baby whatever happened between Paul and I, I came to a place in my head that was entirely unexpected. It was a subtle but definite shift in focus: from myself and the situation

I had managed to get myself into, to the tiny life that was now growing inside me and the responsibility I had for its welfare. I decided that perhaps my becoming a mother was meant to be, after all. That destiny had simply mapped out my life and that I should stop trying to fight the path set for me.

I felt calmer then, knowing that this was one thing that I didn't have to think about any more. Whatever happened with Paul and I now, I was going to become a mother, and who knew? Perhaps a baby would change him for the better. Perhaps a baby was exactly what he needed to make him grow up. And if not, then I would manage. I'd be a single parent, but I'd manage. Just thinking that was an enormous source of comfort.

There was no comfort to be had for me now, however. Without a mother or an auntie or an older, more experienced sister, I was ignorant about almost everything to do with childbirth and babies, despite dutifully attending every antenatal class on offer. So the world of pain and anxiety I now found myself in was truly shocking. Having an episiotomy was excruciating, trying to breastfeed was excruciating, the most sensitive part of my body felt like it had been attacked by a machete, and I was woozy and disorientated through lack of sleep. And fixed in the centre of this universe of bewildered wretchedness was this tiny helpless being - one who was depending upon me to fulfil her every need.

I was useless at doing so in every way. With every movement causing shock waves of pain in my pelvis, every aspect of caring for this only hours old infant perplexed and distressed me. I knew just one thing; that you must always support a baby's head. With cotton wool now in the place where I used to have a brain, that was the sum total of the wisdom that I seemed to be able to call to mind. I had never picked up a baby, so I didn't know how to hold one. I couldn't seem to tap into the 'miracle' of breastfeeding either. I had naïvely assumed that, it being something that was 'natural', it was a process that would happen naturally too.

It wasn't. Neither of us had the first clue how to do it and our early attempts at the business of latching on were so inept that the pain in my left breast was only matched in intensity by the volume of my nameless baby's hungry screams. I tried again and again to get it right that first night, adding guilt and shame to the ever growing list of my disaffections, for causing such a rumpus in the otherwise silent ward and bringing the wrath of the night sister down on my head.

Changing the nappy was a fantastic catastrophe as well. Under different circumstances I would have ended up having a fit of the giggles but there was nothing I felt like laughing about at the moment. In fact, I cried. The first obstacle was the suit she was wearing – and which I'd bought – and which now seemed completely mystifying. There seemed to be press studs everywhere and I pinged a few open, hoping the mystery would unravel itself as I did. No such luck. By the time I had adequate access to the nappy my baby was almost completely naked – not a state of affairs she much liked.

The next challenge was getting the nappy off. This was all uncharted territory, and, in a rush of impetuosity, I whisked the whole thing away from under her, revealing what looked like a mass of black tar, which was now covering pretty much everything. I panicked as another baby fact popped into my brain. That breastfed babies were supposed to have sweet-smelling yellow poo. What was wrong with her that this foul-smelling goo had come out of her? Did she have some sort of hideous disease?

An angel stopped by then; a kind, smiling nurse – the first smile I'd seen since the previous day. She reassured me the goo was normal and soothed me about my ineptitude and did in twenty seconds what it had taken me a full twenty minutes to achieve, explaining each step as she did so, and making it look so ridiculously easy that I felt even more useless than ever.

'You mustn't get upset,' she said, so gently that it made fresh tears plop onto my cheeks. 'Why would you expect to be good at something you've never done before?'

She then handed me the baby so she could clean out the cot and change the bedding and with that done we placed her back in her cot.

'Why don't you go and get some breakfast now,' the nurse suggested. 'It's important you keep your strength up.'

So I did. Despite feeling so dizzy that I thought I'd fall over, I set off. Perhaps I would feel better if I had something to eat. I crept down the ward, step by agonising step, holding the wall, only to find that the breakfast room was full of other mothers, all bouncing around as if nothing much had happened to them. Forget the baby – did *I* have some hideous disease? Why did I feel so terrible, so weak?

It would be a good while before I found out. In the meantime, any chance of rest was immediately scuppered by the arrival of Paul, who was naturally as excited as any new father would be before the reality I'd just lived through for the last 24 hours began to be a reality for him too. He also informed me that his parents would be along to visit a couple of hours later, which only served to fill me with gloom. I'd never been good enough in the eyes of his mother, and my ineptitude now would only serve to confirm it.

I felt so weak, and when Paul's parent's duly arrived, I was at least grateful that his mother spent the whole afternoon holding the baby and doing what I guess all new grandmothers do; wondering at her new toy. Meanwhile I was feeling worse and worse. I barely had the strength to sit up in bed, nevermind feed and change a new baby. And the following morning, after a night in which I'd doggedly continued to breastfeed despite the pain, I felt so weak that I couldn't even get out of bed, let alone stagger down to the breakfast room.

I felt so bad, in fact, that I decided I must be dying, and when, mid-morning, someone came to take routine post-natal blood, I just lay there inert and uncaring. That must be it, I decided, I was fading away. I knew I'd not been cut out for motherhood and this confirmed it – it had literally finished me off.

I drifted off to sleep then, only to be awoken an hour later by some sort of commotion in the corridor outside. The door burst open then, admitting a harried looking doctor. 'Stay in bed,' he ordered. And I was able to reassure him on that point.

'I have no choice,' I told him, 'because I don't think I can move.'

He looked even more concerned and told me that all was not well. 'Your blood iron count,' he explained, 'is only 5.3.'

I didn't know a lot about blood iron counts but, having gone through a pregnancy, I did know that mine was normally about 14, and that 5.3 sounded very low indeed. 'Dangerously low,' the doctor confirmed, going on to inform me that they needed to give me a blood transfusion as a matter of urgency. 'Four units,' he said, 'and it'll take around an hour for the blood to be matched. And in the meantime you are not to move so much as an inch.'

I felt strangely cheered by this news. Finally I had a reason why I felt at death's door! And once I was set up with my bag of blood and my drip, I was even more cheered to find that the brusque nurses who'd effectively been telling me to 'suck it up' for the last two days were now running around attending to my every need.

The only upsetting aspect was that, as I was forbidden to breastfeed for the 24 hours it would take for the transfusion, my daughter was taken away to be given a bottle. It felt so unfair, after we'd both soldiered on so doggedly – not to mention finally getting the hang of it - that she'd be getting something other than my milk after all.

But it clearly wasn't an option, and at least I'd be soon be feeling better. And by the time Paul arrived later that morning, and I was halfway through the first unit of blood, I was also pleased to see the expression of shock on his face. He was even sympathetic, expressing concern for my health and wellbeing and allowing a kernel of hope to lodge in my mind that having this child might just represent a turning point. I was also childishly looking forward to seeing his mother, and to what she might think of my new fashion accessory of a drip stand. Exhausted as I'd been, I hadn't missed her barbed comment the previous day that when they'd lived in Singapore (they'd lived there for a couple of years when Paul was a baby) the women would have their babies and then immediately return to working in the paddy fields.

Well, good for them, I'd thought. Not that I'd have responded, however readily the words 'I'd like to see you try' sprung to my lips, because I'd known her long enough to know it would be pointless. No, the blood transfusion would make the point for me so much better – that I hadn't been making a big fuss about nothing after all.

The transfusion complete, I was allowed to breastfeed again, too, and also given the news that the baby and I would have to stay in for four more days so that they could monitor my anaemia. And I was happy. I was keen to stay as long as they were happy to have me, frankly, because the thought of going home and being alone with my still name-less daughter terrified me, as did the fear that 'maternal' was something I was never going to feel.

But whatever happened now, on one point I was clear. Forget all my intentions about not having an only child. I would *never* get pregnant again.

Chapter Twelve

THE GAME OF
THE NAME

I arrived home with the baby to find Paul had made a 'welcome home' sign for us. His dad was a civil service draughtsman and I recognised the paper – it was from one of the huge rolls he'd periodically let us have for the business. It was around eight feet long and Paul had attached it to the side wall of the big shed in the parking area, along with a couple of bunches of multi-coloured balloons, which were bobbing gaily in the fresh summer breeze. It was a lovely gesture and as he grinned and tooted the horn to let his parents know we'd arrived, I felt the traumas of the last few days melting away. He was so puppyishly delighted, so attentive, so full of smiles that I even felt a rush of optimism about our future. Perhaps, despite all the sage advice counselling that such things didn't happen, this baby might see an end to our relationship traumas and be the catalyst that encouraged a new closeness between us. Perhaps, as a family, we'd be able to move forward together.

Climbing out of the car, however, reminded me forcibly of the physical trauma the birth had wrought, and for all that

I felt lighter of heart, I was exhausted. What I most wanted to do was go straight indoors, feed the baby and have a very long lie down. But Paul, who couldn't have been more excited to welcome his firstborn child home, had other ideas. It was a bright and cloudless day – perfect for the taking of family pictures - so he decided we needed to embark on an hour long photo opportunity on the doorstep, getting shots of me with the baby, him with the baby, both of us with the baby and his parents with the baby - they were naturally there as well – before we were allowed to go inside.

Once in there, however, my face fell. Paul had been hard at work there as well, in one of the ways he knew best; re-arranging all the furniture. So what I saw when we went into the living room was that it had apparently also become my bedroom. 'So you won't have to be up and down the stairs carrying the baby all day,' he explained. 'And it means you'll still be in the thick of things, won't it? Where help will be on hand.'

Again, I accepted the gesture for what I thought it was; a kind and thoughtful one, with my welfare – particularly given the scare about my iron levels – uppermost in Paul's mind. And though I was again pleased, because such thoughtfulness was such a rare and precious thing to me, what I craved most right now was privacy – a sanctuary I could retreat to - particularly as his parents would be staying with us for several days, and friends would also be popping in and out.

There was nothing for it, however, but to accept the arrangements gracefully, however awkward or uncomfortable the set-up. And it was certainly awkward; when I lying was in bed (I struggled to sit, because of my many, many stitches) I felt like a Victorian duchess holding an audience. And with my twin life-savers being a Red Cross donated rubber ring and medicinal Arnica for the bruising, the irony of the similarities wasn't lost on me.

Our baby remained nameless till the last day we could legally register her birth. I had been keen to call her Casey from the outset, but Paul refused to even consider it, and until we could find a name we agreed on we were in dead-lock. And, amid the blur of exhaustion, sleepless nights, and days that were now dominated by the trauma of colic, what to call this tiny being that had entered our lives and turned everything upside down, was the last thing on our minds. But as the weeks passed, and the registry office deadline loomed ever closer, we began amassing an ever-growing pile of baby name books. None seemed to help. It was completely by chance that the solution arrived.

I was trying to breastfeed our fractious infant when a programme came on the television featuring an inspira-tional man in Rio who'd devoted his life to saving the city's orphaned children; the ones who'd taken to living in the sewers. His first name was Jaime, the Spanish version of Jamie, and, as moved as I was by both the children's plight and the commitment and dedication of the man himself, Paul immediately declared Jamie to be the perfect name for our daughter.

'And after Jamie Lee Curtis as well,' he added, by way of an exited afterthought. Which made me smile. He'd always loved Jamie lee Curtis, so this seemed to seal it;

Jamie it would be. Except not quite, as he then added, 'but what about the name Jodie?'

'What about it?' I asked him as I tried to settle the object of our discussion for yet another attempt at feeding. 'I thought we'd already agreed on Jamie?'

'Yes, but I like Jodie too, so why not have both?'

'You mean as a second name?' I asked him.

He shook his head. 'No. As in joining them together, with a hyphen.'

I tried it on my tongue. 'Jamie-Jodie?' It felt a bit of a mouthful, to my mind. And wouldn't everyone end up calling her Jamie anyway?

But Paul thought it was perfect so, needless to say, when we went down to register our daughter's birth the following morning, the name on the certificate was indeed Jamie-Jodie.

At the time of Jamie's birth, it still hadn't occurred to me that Paul might have mental health issues. I persisted in the belief that when he behaved strangely, or aggressively, or abused me emotionally, it must surely in some way be my fault for 'handling' him all wrong. I had been extremely well-programmed to do so. Paul's dominance and ability to bend me constantly to his will was nothing I hadn't seen before. The way he was with me was no different from the way my father had been with my mother; and my mother – to my child's eye, at any rate, until her untimely death when I was a teenager – had meekly accepted his domestic tyranny as her lot.

Their situation, of course, was very different from ours; looked at objectively, their marriage was a terrible mess, wobbling above foundations set in the unstable quicksand of infidelity, lies and guilt. But without a mother, an out-side view, a clear-sighted analysis of how Paul and I fitted together, meek acceptance seemed to be my default set-ting too. Not because I *felt* meek, or even weak – it was just that the concept of breaking free was one that no longer seemed to apply. No, better to find ways to make it work – that was my mantra. To conduct myself in such a way that Paul was content and we could live in relative harmony.

Rationally, even then, I was perfectly aware of Paul's failings, even if he refused to accept that he had any. I knew very well that he had been spoilt by his doting mother. I was all too aware that his charisma eclipsed his shortcom-ings; that there were two sides to this outwardly charming man. But there was that constant in my make-up that kept my conviction very strong that if he wasn't happy in the relationship, it *must* be my fault. I must be dealing with him all wrong – it was a thought I had regularly. Just as my mother had wrestled with the same basic mindset, just as every night, when my father came home from work, the atmosphere would become unbearable, just as my mother would become tense and not-quite-herself and appeas-ing, so it was with Paul and I – unless *I* could change. In short, I wasn't quite managing to do what his mother kept reminding me; everything I could to make him happy.

It feels insane, looking back, because hindsight is a wonderful thing, and I don't doubt there are women for whom such notions of inadequacy seem incredible. But I'm sure there will be other women who know exactly what I'm talking about. Who jump through hoops, in a state of high-anxiety and terrible tension, to try and maintain the holy grail of peace and harmony; who mod-ify their behaviour in an effort not to be shouted at.

That was me as a child, moulded in my dead mother's image. That it might be that it was actually Paul who was dif-ficult, emotionally damaged, mentally fragile, mentally *ill*… I was still too busy trying to please him to even consider it.

Though our family had grown, it had also now grown smaller. By the time we brought Jamie home Paul had got rid of all but one of our remaining dogs, largely by stealth. Having agreed to him putting them in kennels just for a couple of weeks while the baby 'settled', I had already endured the loss of Hobo – being so elderly, the move had effectively killed him. And when Jamie was just a few weeks old, I was now faced with the news that BJ wouldn't be coming home either. While in the care of the Dogs Trust, he'd been spotted by an elderly couple who'd recently lost their own beloved Jack Russell, and wanted to take him on. And, having received the enquiry, Paul had gone ahead and organised everything, leaving me, when I was put in the picture about where BJ had gone, feeling unable to rock their world again by demanding we have him back.

It was only Spring who returned (perhaps predictably, because Paul adored her) and I couldn't have been more ecstatic about being reunited with her. She also immediately took to Jamie – a situation that would very soon become mutual. Within weeks of being home again her preferred place to sleep was curled up next to Jamie's Moses basket.

By this time, our growing business had shrunk some-what as well. Not in terms of business itself – between us, we were steadily building something solid – but in terms of staff, of which there were now just two - us. Though we had a number of guys who worked on a freelance basis for us, the few staff we'd employed had never lived up to Paul's exacting expectations, and he'd decided we were better off without them. Which meant there was nothing for it but for me to get back to work as soon as I was physically able.

This was to prove no mean feat. As a new mother, without benefit of a circle of more experienced female relatives, I found the day-to-day business of caring for the baby difficult enough in itself. And with the need to return to work full-time while adjusting to the seismic shift in our lives thrown in, neither of us were coping at all well.

Here at least, Paul's mother came into her own. With events to organise and run all over the country, Paul often felt he needed me with him, to run the 'people' side of things, particularly if the events were very big ones. He would therefore draft in his mother to allow this to happen, expecting her to look after Jamie, often late into the night, even though I was breastfeeding, which made it hard for all of us. I would try to find ways around going, because I knew Paul would cope perfectly well without me once he got used to it, but both he and his mother would be adamant. As ever, her main concern was that Paul had no stress, even if it meant her spending long hours with a frazzled, hungry baby, which only served to highlight just how inadequate *I* was. I didn't doubt then, and I still don't doubt now, that she thought I was an extremely poor mother.

It wasn't just me who was struggling with the demands of work and parenthood however. Paul, who'd been so desperate to father lots of children was, like many fathers, finding the reality rather sobering. There was also the business of us running our business from home, creating problems that were trying his patience to the limit, and inspiring him to try and come up with solutions.

There is no 'solution' to the business of caring for a baby. They require your commitment, your ability to meet their physical and emotional demands and, most of all, they require your attention. I learned this quickly and I understood it rationally. I was a mother, and now that I felt it in my heart as well as my head, it was attention I also ached to give her. But this was at odds with the work that needed to be done for the business, so, in Paul's eyes, a 'solution' to this problem needed to be found.

By this time we had acquired a baby bouncer; one of those contraptions you can attach to a door frame and then sit the baby in so that, secured to the frame by means of a harness slung between two lengths of strong elastic, the baby can move their legs and effectively bounce. We'd not used it much, as Jamie hadn't shown much interest in it; she was a fractious baby and would soon tire of being 'amused' by such things when what she wanted was to be with her mother.

Looking back it was ridiculous expecting her to be – something every mother learns in the end. If you need to work, then you need childcare out of sight of where you're working. No normal infant, when awake, is going to do anything but get upset when they are in full sight of their mum but not allowed to interact with her. And as there was no one else to care for her, there *was* no solution to this. But that didn't stop Paul from trying to find one.

'I've got an idea!' he exclaimed one day while we were both trying to do paperwork and he was getting agitated as usual. We'd tried to settle her – every nap was like a gift from on high – but she was six months old now and she just wasn't tired. What I really needed to do was down tools and attend to her, but that 'solution' was out of the question.

He dashed off without waiting for an answer and returned moments later with a hammer and a handful of four-inch nails. He then proceeded to bang two of them high into the doorframe at a 45 degree angle. I was mystified, wondering what he was about to do, and even more so when he plonked Jamie into the bouncer's harness.

I didn't have to wait for long. Before I knew it, he had lifted her skywards and slung the harness between the nails, six feet from the floor.

'You can't do that!' I gasped, horrified to see my bemused infant dangling up there, looking down at me. 'You can't hang her up there from two *nails*! Supposing they give way?'

'It's perfectly safe,' Paul said, demonstrating his confidence in his contraption by tugging hard on Jamie's leg. 'See? Safe as houses. And look – she's enjoying it. She'll be fine. Stop fussing. We can get some work done now.'

He was right about that. Jamie's new vantage point was clearly holding her attention as was the sensation of having her legs dangling in space. But though Paul had made his point, I was far too anxious to concentrate for the next 15 minutes, and breathed a sigh of relief when she tired of that too and started screaming and wriggling with sufficient commitment that Paul had no choice but get her back down. Looking back now, as with so much, I'm horrified that I allowed him to do it in the first place.

Other ideas he had started out being more conventional. His other main containment measure (of which there would be all sorts over several years and children) was a huge playpen he constructed in the office. We worked out of the extension – a space the previous owners had used as a farm shop – and he spent days building the structure. When complete it was some eight by eight foot square. Needless to say, when he first plonked Jamie down in the middle of it, however, she just sat there and screamed. We'd filled it with toys and, now she bum-shuffled, she could move around and get to them, but she didn't want to do that – like any baby she wanted to play with us, and would simply hold out both her chubby arms and sob for me.

I'm not sure if a better form of torture has ever been devised, but Paul was adamant that if we let her cry she'd soon become used to the arrangement and, with my ignorance of all things to do with babies, I would let him browbeat me into believing that he might just know best, even though today the idea seems so risible.

He was right about one thing, that we needed to work to earn sufficient money to keep a roof over our heads and with only his mother to help out with childcare when we were both required to do an event, we had no choice but to endure it.

It was certainly true that when he decided that perhaps she ought to go into a nursery every afternoon, I felt it was probably the right thing to do. Much as it broke my heart – five hours away every day seemed so long for such a tiny child – a part of me also felt relieved for her. She might miss us, but she would surely have much more fun than she currently was at home. I understood how she felt.

Chapter Thirteen
BABY STEPS

As soon as I'd recovered from the worst of the shock of new parenthood, I decided to abandon my 'never again' stance, and return to the thinking that had dominated throughout the pregnancy; that Paul and I should try to have another baby. For all that I had been struggling – with the business, with motherhood and, as ever, with Paul's Jekyll and Hyde-like and increasingly erratic behaviour - I had this powerful feeling that Jamie mustn't be an only child. It was the legacy of my own childhood, I suppose; I'd longed so much for a sister. And now, apart from my infant daughter, I really felt I had no one in the world; a father who wasn't really my father, a brother who had abused me, another who was too autistic to leave home and with whom I could barely communicate, and, in Paul's mother, at least, an in-law that felt not so much an extended family as the enemy at the gate, even when she was helping us out.

Whenever Jean and John were around I always had this sense that they were waiting to pounce on anything I did that they didn't agree with. This was particularly true of Jean, whose constant hovering and relentlessly disapproving presence had, since Jamie's birth, become a thorn in my side, even while, paradoxically, I felt so enormously grateful for the support. They would come to stay with us two weekends out of four, even though they were both still working (John full time), mostly to babysit while Paul dragged me to interminable business meetings for a firm called Amway – an American business he'd bought into, and which he was convinced would be the way we were going to make our fortune. And when it came to his mother, particularly, we shared an unlikely meeting of minds; Paul would get very cross if she ever suggested they might go home a bit earlier on a Sunday night than had originally been the plan. And she never stood up to him, either.

I decided to return to the doctor when Jamie was coming up to a year old, and was prescribed the drug Clomid to help me conceive. My doctor had already told me that the odds of my conceiving again naturally were virtually zero; quite apart from the problems that had dogged me since puberty, I apparently also had a tilted uterus and various other problems with my fallopian tubes. Conceiving Jamie had obviously been something of a miracle.

There was also the business of having a demanding little human around as well, of course, but now she was attending nursery, I felt on a much more even keel, especially as I'd begun building a support network of other mothers. None were particularly close; I felt the same sense of being an outsider as I'd done as a child and teenager, a feeling that was probably enhanced by the fact that we lived such isolated lives. But there was one girl I felt close to, ironically called Vicki, the wife of Brian, one of

Paul's 'friends' from the local pub. Curiously – though, with hindsight, entirely in character – it was a closeness Paul was always keen to discourage, but she felt like the first real friend I'd made since we'd moved to the Midlands.

The business was thriving as well. With me being able to work longer hours, knowing Jamie was being well cared for, gave me a valuable sense of fulfilment and wellbeing. All in all, it felt as if life held a great deal more promise; that motherhood would ultimately give me a new strength and purpose. Which was good because, despite our rickety relationship and my very shaky start at motherhood, I knew I was going to hang in there and make it work, come hell or high water.

Paul couldn't have been more delighted. Which in one sense was inexplicable, since he seemed to find one child so challenging. But it also marked the start of a period of relative harmony between us; one that resulted in the news, when Jamie was just approaching two, that I was going to have another baby.

I should have anticipated that the peace wasn't to last. Once I was pregnant again, it was as if Paul underwent a personality transplant, and he began disappearing on a regular basis.

At first, it didn't tend to be that far. Back when I'd been pregnant with Jamie, we'd bought a motorhome for the business, which, along with a trailer, could be used sometimes in place of one of the vans. I'd been very reluctant, mostly because of the extra expense, but Paul's idea in this case did have some logic. Once I'd had the second baby, he reasoned, I'd be able to attend and run fewer events, particularly those that were a long way away. Travelling alone, he reasoned, it would be much more economical for him to sleep in the motorhome than have to stay overnight in costly hotels.

So far, he'd used it a grand total of once, so it had mostly been quietly rusting in the yard, leaching cash. Now, however, he found another use for it. He would sometimes drive it to the middle of one of the fields and park it, then hole up there alone for a couple of days, doing whatever he did in there, only returning to the house when Jamie and I were out. His other 'bolt-hole' when family life became to much for him was, perhaps predictably, his parents' home – he'd had a habit of stomping out and returning there in the aftermath of a row since we'd first been together.

He was still doing it now, sometimes after an argument but, increasingly, it seemed to be for no reason that I could fathom, except that of simply being unable to cope with his parental responsibilities. He wouldn't be the first man on the planet to have done so, after all. What his parents thought of this was never discussed – not with me, anyway.

Paul, for all his desperation to have a large family, seemed pathologically ill-suited to family life, full stop. And I wasn't just used to him disappearing for days at a time; at times I was even grateful that he did so, as well, as it gave me a respite from trying to tiptoe around his temper. But it was a need that was clearly becoming almost a compulsion, as evidenced by what I found when I was around 15 weeks pregnant.

Soon after we'd moved into the house, Paul had erected a wooden shed in the small parking area next to the house. It was huge as sheds went – around 25 feet by 20 – and its purpose had been both to act as a workshop for construction and repairs and provide storage space for all the games equipment.

No more. One day he gutted it – emptied it of every single thing in it, and transferred it all to one of the barns. Now the shed was empty, he started spending much of his time there when he wasn't out doing events, and I could constantly hear banging and the sound of power tools being used. I had no idea what he was up to and not for a minute would I have thought of asking him; I knew he'd only lie to me or get annoyed that I was questioning him, and above all – as was becoming the way we mostly lived – I would do anything I could to avoid sparking any sort of row. So I left him to it, and he'd soon only appear very sporadically, returning to the house only to make himself his endless cups of tea. He'd say almost nothing - though he'd give Jamie a cursory' hello' if she was home from nursery, that was pretty much it. He wouldn't even look at me.

This kind of behaviour was far from rare so, though it was irksome, it didn't overly concern me. He'd be doing what he always did – hiding himself away to make some piece of equipment or other for the business, or he'd be engaged in some mad scheme I would doubtless hear about eventually – usually only by the time he'd spent money we didn't have on something that was unlikely to make us any either. But as the days went on, it was inevitable that my curiosity would be aroused sufficiently to make me wonder exactly what was going on in there.

The only trouble was that he kept the building locked at all times, so I wasn't quite sure how I'd be able to get in and see. I had to hope for some luck, and started keeping a closer eye on his comings and goings, hoping that at some point he'd nip out and forget to lock up, enabling me to nip across and see what I could see.

It took several days but eventually my patience was rewarded. Paul was so anal and particular that I despaired of him ever being so sloppy, but one day, about a week after I'd first been keeping an eye on his comings and goings, I realised he'd driven off leaving the door unlocked. It was entirely out of character, and it was also my chance, so I hot-footed it across the yard to see what I could see.

It was with no small amount of trepidation that I peered into the interior, however – I was terrified that he might return at any moment and become incandescent that I'd dared take a look. But I was reasonably confident that I would hear the sound of the van coming back down the lane, so I finally dared open the door a little wider and step inside.

What I saw was at first just confusing. What had previously been one enormous space had now been divided; where previously I would have walked into a cavernous space, I now found myself in a thin corridor, its walls made of plywood, that seemed to run the whole length of the shed. Where there had once been a single room, it now seemed there were several; there were openings at the end of the corridor that seemed to lead off left and right.

Because we'd long ago boarded up the windows so that potential thieves couldn't see the valuable tools and equipment that had previously been stored there, it was very dark inside. The only light source was that which was spilling in from the open door, so I walked gingerly down the narrow corridor, the resiny smell of plywood sharp in my nostrils, fearful of what I might find at its end, and equally fearful that Paul might come back and find me. I reached the end, chose the right turn, and found myself on another short corridor which led to a small open area. I gazed around me, mildly intrigued to see what looked like a makeshift kitchen. There was a kettle I didn't recognise, together with a couple of mugs and plates which I did, and it suddenly came to me that in the last couple of days the number of visits indoors for cups of tea had reduced considerably.

There was a short corridor leading off from this area as well, so I headed off down it. Here I found another area, this one very obviously an office. I had a double-take here as well. Stationed at a makeshift desk that he'd obviously built himself was an armchair from the house that had recently, and mysteriously, disappeared.

Not that furniture disappearing was an oddity in itself. Such furniture as we had was often subject to Paul's periodic clear-outs and late-night rearrangements. It wasn't unusual to come down in the morning to find the living room had become the dining room overnight, and he had already stripped out and rearranged the kitchen more than once. He had also by now ripped out a big internal wall to create a studio from two adjoining bedrooms. It was as if he felt compelled to keep streamlining and de-cluttering our home; to create a cavernous, minimalist environment.

Here in the shed, however, was its antithesis. The interior he had painstakingly created was like a maze and as I retraced my steps, in order to take the left branch of the central corridor, I was having difficulty taking in the scale of it. So he hadn't been building or repairing equipment at all; he'd been creating a warren within the empty shed's shell.

Having returned to the central corridor I headed down another, and after two turns, found myself in a bedroom. It could be seen as nothing else. There was a mattress on the floor which he'd made up with bedding from indoors, complete with a bedside table on which stood one of the extendable lamps we used for events. There was even a clothes rail, on which various items of his clothing were neatly hung.

I was totally bewildered by the oddity of it all. What on earth was he doing? He had turned the interior of the shed into his own private quarters – it put me in mind of the sort of secret bunker you read about in books about war; it felt almost like an animal's lair.

I returned to the house and within less than a minute Paul reappeared, not coming into the house but going straight into the shed. It was all so bizarre I felt even less inclined to ask him about it than I had previously; it was a watershed moment in my understanding of his nature – perhaps the first time it came to me, rationally and unemotionally, that the man I married wasn't right in the head. Put to anyone outside the strange world we inhabited in private, it would surely have seemed bizarre in the extreme. And even more bizarre was that within a couple of days of my discovery, he took to sleeping there every night as well, and communicating with me mostly via the written word. I would return from taking Jamie to nursery to find long lists of things to do for the business, all written neatly in his tiny, meticulous writing, and complete with spaces in which I was to write down each outcome.

My world shifted very slightly off its axis at that point. What was I to make of such behaviour? And more to the point, what was I to do about it? I could challenge it; I could ask Paul why he felt the need to live this way, yet - equally bizarrely, perhaps - that was the one thing I felt least able to do.

Leave. That was the word that kept flashing up in my brain as I lay sleepless in the marital bed that night. This was surely not a sane way to live. It kept coming back to me, too; so much so that in the next couple of weeks I even went as far as looking at a couple of flats in nearby Kenilworth where Jamie and I might live. I might have found the wherewithal to take her and disappear myself, too, except that something kept stopping me. Some part of me seemed to take precedence over every objective thought; deep down I knew that Paul's behaviour was far from normal, but, perhaps fuelled more by fear of the unknown than the known, I kept explaining away his behaviour as him just 'being a man' and 'retreating into his cave'. After all, it was just a version of how my father had treated my mother some of the time; all bonhomie and personality when out in the wider world, but ignoring her (and us) when behind closed doors.

And it wasn't hard for Paul to keep up the pretence. We had very few visitors, and when any did turn up he would either appear from it, as if from working, or simply remain holed up inside till they'd gone again. But the final nail in the coffin of any unformed plan to leave came when I was around five months pregnant. A letter came through telling Paul that there was finally a date for him to have the operation he so craved - to try and do something about the deformity in his penis that had dogged him (and perhaps his psyche?) all his adult life. He'd been on the waiting list for quite a while and had already had two prior dates cancelled, and crossed everything that this one wouldn't be cancelled too.

It wasn't. And once again, our relationship changed completely. After what ended up being around two months of him sleeping almost exclusively in the shed, he returned to the house as if nothing odd had occurred and seemed to set about trying to make things up with me. And when the operation was over, I allowed myself to be optimistic about the future. Perhaps the surgery would also help heal the damage to his sense of masculinity – it must have been a difficult thing for a man to have to live with after all.

That was what I was good at; seeing the best. Hoping for the best. Because, though I knew him well enough to realise he was probably just feeling vulnerable and in need of emotional support, I seemed incapable of understanding that it would surely only be a matter of time before the old Paul returned to bully me anew.

Chapter Fourteen
THE AMERICAN WAY

Our second daughter, Kacie-Kimie, was born in December 1993, and once again choosing her name was a problem. I was still keen on the name Casey, which he'd refused to countenance the last time, but Paul still wouldn't entertain it. 'How can we do that?' he wanted to know, incredulous. 'It begins with a C. Jamie's started with a J, so this one has to start with a K.'

As with most things, his plan did have the benefit of logic, the logic being that we must now follow certain rules. We had to continue along the alphabet and, now he'd seized on another potential pattern, the new baby's name must also consist of two names, totalling ten letters, just as Jamie's had – five and five, separated by a hyphen.

Luckily for me, he was happy if Casey was spelt Kacie, not least because his research – and he did lots of that – showed that 'Kacie' meant 'brave' in Irish. Kimie was straightforward too, the same book flagging up that it meant 'the best', this time in Japanese.

It's so clear to me now; the guiding principle by which Paul tried to live his life; the constant need to create some sort of pattern where there was none; to do all within his power to create order out of chaos. The chaos that increasingly threatened to overwhelm his head. And where I failed to grasp so much of this while I was trying to live alongside it, with Kacie's birth came the realisation that I too needed to create order – it being the only way I could find a way through the maelstrom of early motherhood, and the constant struggle of trying to fit too much into way too few hours.

By the time Kacie-Kimie was about four months old, and Jamie was a spirited and energetic two year old, I pleaded with Paul to find a way to release me from my work commitments, just enough so that I could concentrate - if only temporarily - on being a mother. 'But *why* can't you cope?' he demanded when I tried to broach this. 'Other working mothers manage perfectly well!'.

I kept trying to explain that other working mothers usually went *to* their place of work – and had their children looked after while they were gone. He still didn't accept this, but in the end he came up with a solution anyway – we should just sell the business. He'd been muttering about doing this for a while already, anyway, having become convinced that his future lay in Amway, the American network marketing business (Amway is short for 'American Way') which he thought was the greatest thing ever, and to whose meetings he had been dragging me to since Jamie had been a baby.

Amway, looking back, might have been the beginning of the end in many ways. A huge multi-level marketing business, in the cleaning, health, beauty and wellbeing sectors, Paul was obsessed with it – and for a number of years, as well. He also bought into it at a time when it was getting a lot of terrible press, as the consensus seemed to be that it was an illegal pyramid scheme. In fact, it wasn't, but there's no doubt that people were extremely wary of it during that period, which contributed negatively to what would probably have happened anyway; Paul sinking huge amounts of money we didn't have into trying to make a go of it, and failing to match evangelical levels of enthusiasm with the sort of action that would translate into income.

In the short term, it certainly contributed to imminent financial meltdown, as Paul's response to my concerns about how I was going to look after two babies and work full time for our games business was to sell it and throw all our time and resources into Amway instead. He bought into the whole concept, lock stock and barrel, joining an Amway group that, hilariously, was called IBS - though in this case not an acronym for the gut-churning financial anxiety that was ever a part of it, but Independent Business Systems. The philosophy of IBS, as with much that Amway peddled, was based on Positive Thinking, archaic beliefs that the man was THE BOSS (there being certain things that women, as part of an IBS couple, were not allowed to do) and a degree of good old-fashioned brainwashing. Though not brainwashed by Amway, I must have been brainwashed by Paul's enthusiasm because I just shut up, supported him and hoped for the best. Perhaps it was the solution to our business problems. Who was I to say?

But Paul's obsession with Amway came at a terrible business cost. Without my knowing, he then called up a regular client and, just as he had with buying the house, 'negotiated' a terrible deal. I could hardly believe it. The whole thing made no sense to me anyway, and here he was, virtually giving our company away. Worse than that, the deal included us continuing working for the business as well as Amway – the upshot being that we would now work just as hard, even harder, for less money.

Yet, inexplicably, in the midst of this, after coming across some old clomid tablets, he decided – and there would be no shutting him up on the matter – that we needed to try for another baby. We were having almost no sex by this point, but that would all obviously have to change, because, as I already knew from my experience with having Kacie, he would be as goal-orientated about this as about anything.

And I agreed. Looking back, it seems incredible. Utter madness. And as I write today I keep hearing a voice in my own head shouting 'Vikie, what were you *thinking*?' But at the time, there was a certain logic to my actions, however skewed that form of logic seems now. I remember calculating the odds, almost dispassionately. It had taken many, many months for me to fall pregnant with Kacie using Clomid, and as I was breast-feeding full-time, and not having periods, the chances of my conceiving seemed infinitesimal. This weighing up of pros and cons was key to so much of my thinking during my marriage – trying to balance the unknown negatives that might be the result of doing what Paul wanted, with the all-too-well known negative of actively defying him; a fight.

But I was wrong. In early July, within two weeks of agreeing to take the clomid, I began to feel a familiar sensation and I knew that against some incredible odds, I could well be – probably was – pregnant once again.

I went and got a pregnancy testing kit, trying to hope against hope that my gut instinct might, just this once, be wrong. But it wasn't my lucky day and I was shaken rigid to see the line indicate a positive, and the thought of terminating it quickly flashed into my mind. But the maternal instinct that I never thought would be part of my chemistry soon kicked such ideas into touch. I had two children already, so how hard could a third be? And besides, I shouldn't have been such a bloody idiot in the first place. No, this baby deserved to survive.

I remember the evening I broke the news well. We were all in the dining room, and, since Paul had by now begun his furniture clearance process, the four of us – him and me, Jamie and little Kacie, who were playing – were all sitting on the floor.

I didn't bother with any preamble. 'Guess what? I'm pregnant,' I announced and Paul's response was immediate and electric. He leapt up, grinning from ear to ear, and scooped Jamie into his arms, then proceeded to dance around the room with her.

Jamie was old enough to understand what the word 'baby' meant and was quickly as excited as Paul was, petting my tummy once he'd put her down and given me a hug and told me he was over the moon. 'I can't believe it!' he kept saying, shaking his head. 'I didn't think there was a cat in hell's chance of you conceiving. It's a miracle, Vikie, don't you think? A total miracle!'

He then sat down again, close to me, the smile on his face even wider. 'And you know what this means?' he asked.

I told him I didn't.

'It means that we *have* to get married!'

Chapter Fifteen
TWO BECOME FOUR

24th September 1994

Who was the person who agreed to marry Paul that day? I look back and I'm not sure I know her.

Our wedding took place after a scant six weeks of hurried preparations, following what was possibly a candidate for the longest engagement in history. Paul had actually asked me to marry him within a few months of us moving in together and I had said yes. He'd bought me an engagement ring which had long since been consigned to my jewelry box and whilst I never referred to him as my fiancé (and neither did he) it was a kind of accepted thing that one day we would eventually get married and make everything legal.

After years during which it hadn't even been mentioned, I agreed partly in the interests of security. Though there was no difference between two and three children, any more than there was between two and a dozen, the children did make a difference to me. And it was nothing to do with what I'd worked out was Paul's primary motivation, either - the Amway way of having strong 'family values'. No, the children simply meant that I was tied to Paul for life, and the rational head that still clung on my shoulders – however precariously – knew that being married could only make my financial position stronger.

If I was unemotional about the business of being married, which, despite Paul's enthusiasm for it, I largely was, I was still reasonably keen to make my wedding day a nice one, a far as I could. There wasn't a great deal of time to plan – it was arranged and took place within six weeks, but as I wasn't the type to be stressing about seat covers and favours, I was happy enough with what I planned.

The only complicating factor was my fast growing bump. I was 14 weeks pregnant on the day so choosing a dress that would accommodate the already large bump wasn't easy. I went shopping with Paul's mother; we were getting on then as well as we ever had - and I ended up buying the dress in Debenhams in Oxford Street. It wasn't what I would have chosen had I not been pregnant (or, indeed, with Jean, or with my brain firing on all cylinders) because it was a fussy thing – not me at all. But as she liked it so much, and given the price tag attached to it, I bought it anyway. I was only ever planning on getting married the once, so it seemed insane to spend money we didn't have.

It was what can best be described as a bog-standard wedding: I'd organised most of it myself and it was really pretty basic. We had about 60 people for a sit-down meal and then some more in the evening, most of which were our Amway 'friends', and yet more of Paul's family - people I either hardly knew or had never actually met. As had been the case all my life, my own 'family' contingent was tiny; just my father and Brenda, Phillip and his wife, Gillian, my brother Tony (who could have been anywhere) and my mother's brother, Uncle Chris, and his wife, another Brenda.

Still, a wedding was a wedding, and though it wasn't a marriage made in heaven, I did enjoy being dressed up in all my finery, the belle of the ball, in some small way, anyway. Though it was probably optimistic to assume it would go without a hitch, and it didn't – literally.

I'd had my dress altered for me by a local lady and one other thing she'd suggested was to have the means to hook my train up to the skirt for the reception. Unfortunately, however, she'd underestimated the weight of it, and as soon as I duly hooked it up, the hooks and eyes she'd attached promptly ripped off, meaning the train had to be sewn to the dress instead – it was so long, there was no question of leaving it trailing behind me.

This took time, of course, so Paul and I had our first row as newlyweds; instead of going ahead down to the reception, he chose to stay in the hotel room and shout at me. On reflection, this was probably just another manifestation of his curious inability to face the world alone; reminiscent of the times when he'd plead with me to make phone calls to excuse him from things he didn't want to do. But at the time it just meant a miserable start to the reception and the applying of false happy faces when we did go downstairs.

It set a tone and provided a metaphor for the state of our relationship as well; our first dance was to *Three Times a Lady* only because the DJ insisted we had to do one, and neither of us could think of a song that was 'ours'. Incredible, looking back, particularly given that Paul was – or, rather had been, a musician.

But my wedding day was, if not strictly speaking over-shadowed, certainly knocked off the top spot of things on my mind by news we'd had a scant fortnight before it happened. There was a reason why my bump had been swelling so alarmingly and to be grateful for my expand-able dress. Probably as a result of the Clomid, given that there was no history in either family, it turned out that I was expecting not just a third child but a fourth. My scan had shown that I was pregnant with twins.

It couldn't have come at a worse time. With the busi-ness now sold, our finances were dreadful and despite Paul's grand plans for a bright Amway future, we were hanging on pretty much by a thread.

It was particularly galling to be putting in so many hours and having so little to show for it, as well. And despite my pregnancy, there was no question of it letting up. Just after we found out I was carrying twins we had a huge event to do in London which entailed a 24 hour day. I couldn't believe it when Paul told me that he still expected me to be there – we had two strapping lads working for us, who'd be there doing it as well - let alone go in the van and return in the van as well. But it seemed my presence was non-negotiable, because Paul still hated dealing with clients and their staff, and he'd already booked his parents to look after Jamie and Kacie.

It was a gruelling job. I helped to load all of the equip-ment before we drove down there, helped carry it up six flights of stairs, set it all up and then ran the cash desk from 9pm-3am, then helped to dismantle it all and help carry it all back down to the van, ready for driving home to greet the dawn.

This was on the Friday night, and on the Monday, I started bleeding. Examination by our family doctor only revealed one heartbeat, so the beginning of the following week saw me sent straight to the hospital where, happily, a scan showed both the babies were okay. Even so, they kept me in till they were happy everything had settled but it was the start of what would happen for the rest of the pregnancy – me going in and out of hospital with an 'irritable' uterus, being given drugs to stop it contracting, then being allowed home, only to have them start up once again.

I was still trying to help run events with Paul, look after Jamie and Kacie and with the constant back and forth – at one point I was even rushed to Coventry, because they had a neo-natal unit – I was exhausted. It's fair to say that when, at 34 weeks, they couldn't stop the labour, my principal feeling, concern about the premature nature of it notwithstanding, was that if my body was determined to get these twins out then that was definitely alright by me.

It's no wonder I was exhausted, as any mother of young children will understand. There are just over three and half years between the eldest four children and with Kacie being only 13 months old when the twins were born (and not yet able to walk) in practical terms, it wasn't far off having triplets.

I'd had such a difficult (if shortish) labour and though they were six weeks early, they spent the first three of those in special care. But once they were home, and had put on sufficient weight, life looked like returning to normal – well, 'our' normal, anyway, which of course first involved the usual debacle over choosing names.

What I would eventually recognise as being a part of Paul's OCD meant that now he'd come up with his system - two names, hyphenated, with five letters each and 'ie' on the end of both words – we had to observe the rules with the new arrivals. This meant the names available to us were very restricted as one had to be Ls and the other Ms. We discussed it endlessly, getting nowhere until Paul hit on the genius of calling the first Mirie – because it was a miracle she survived her birth – followed by Marie, and that was that – I had no say.

He then started work on the L. It took forever, and, once again, my input was dismissed, with him eventually deciding on Lorie, because its root was the laurel bush, and then Lanie because it sounded like a laurel bush in a lane. I was by now too exhausted to care either way, and was just happy to try and get back into some kind of routine.

But I perhaps should have expected that anything being routine in my life was an unrealistic dream. One day, when the twins were around six weeks old, and I'd fed them both, I put them in their mechanical swings in the next room to rock them to sleep, as per usual. They loved the swings (they were an absolute godsend, and I can't recommend them highly enough) and, leaving them to nod off I returned to the kitchen, where Paul was with the girls. He headed off then, to attend to the VAT return, but before he did, he popped in to check on the babies and called me in, worried that all was not well.

I shared his concern. Mirie didn't look right; she was ashen-faced and motionless. I grabbed her out of the swing and cuddled her but her body was completely limp, and as

I jiggled her up and down to try and get some sign of life from her, I could feel the panic start to rise. Eventually she took a sharp breath and I heaved a sigh of relief, but, even so, we both knew something was badly wrong.

I rang the hospital and was told to bring both babies in immediately, which I did, leaving Paul to look after Jamie and Kacie, and with my heart in mouth the whole way.

I was quickly ushered in to see the doctor, who examined both babies, and quizzed me about whether either were sickly babies.

'Mirie is,' I told him. 'She's always been sickly – she often vomits almost as soon as she's been fed.'

'Projectile vomiting?' he asked me, describing exactly the process we'd often witnessed, where her vomit could be propelled right across the room.

I told him yes, and he decided it would be best to keep both babies in, so they could keep them both under observation, then perhaps take them to Birmingham Children's Hospital for further tests.

These took place a few days later and, for Mirie, they weren't encouraging; she apparently had an extreme case of reflux. This was because the valve at the entrance to her stomach wasn't working properly, so as her stomach digested food the acid wasn't being contained, and everything was coming back up again.

In an adult, we'd call it heartburn; something unpleasant to suffer from, but never life-threatening. In Mirie's case it was a very different story. She was going to need monitoring every minute of her life for as long as was necessary until she was stronger. Crucially, she needed to be strong enough that the reflux didn't cause her to stop breathing.

We were given heart monitors for both babies, just to be on the safe side, which they had to wear at all times. If the reflux caused Mirie to stop breathing, her heart would stop beating, and if this happened the monitor would sound an alarm.

That was only half the picture, obviously. In tandem with that, I was sent on a special CPR course for small babies so that I could revive her if necessary. And it wasn't a case of 'just in case' either. That course saved her life nine times over the next 18 months.

Once we arrived home again a set of professional scales were delivered from the hospital as well. I had to weigh both babies every day, at exactly the same time, before feeding them, because research had apparently shown that babies with severe reflux would often experience a slight weight drop just as they were at a particularly vulnerable stage, and, frighteningly, that they would often die from the consequences. So the hospital organised a home help for me, through social services, and she came to the house for a few hours every day, to help me weigh, bath and feed the twins, help look after the other children and also give me some assistance help with the housework.

I couldn't have been more grateful, because I needed her desperately. I was totally overwhelmed by fear, not to mention exhausted looking after four young children. And as I was breastfeeding the twins, sleep was in incredibly short supply. I lived in a permanent fog not knowing what day of the week it was and permanently on edge wondering when Mirie's next attack would be.

There were false alarms to contend with as well. The alarms would also be set off if the sensor strap moved away from the babies' heartbeat and as they got older and were able to move around more the alarms were constantly going off. This made it all too easy, as they grew, to become a little complacent, a little like when the burglar alarm on a house is constantly being set off, and the neighbours soon stop taking notice.

I learnt to take notice the hard way when they were six months old. I'd put both the babies in their cots for a nap, baby monitor in hand, obviously, and on this particular day, the alarms kept on sounding, so I'd been up and down stairs numerous times.

All was quiet for a few minutes and I thought they must have gone to sleep, so when the alarm went of again but I could hear neither baby crying, I didn't rush. I finished off what I'd been doing and it must have been a couple of minutes before I trotted up.

I walked into their room and it was as if my own heart had stopped. Lorie was sleeping peacefully but Mirie was white and lifeless – a look I knew far too well by now. I ran to the cot and grabbed her, trying to remember the process for reviving her – I'd been here before but it had always been almost instantaneous, so she'd never been anything like this far gone. Knowing that terrified me so much that my training went out of the window and as I held her lifeless body I desperately tried to recall what to do.

It was sheer panic: I was on my own with just Jamie and Kacie in the house and even if Paul had been there, he hadn't done the course anyway. But the panic was then replaced as, suddenly, I felt a peculiar calm engulf me. I laid Mirie gently on the floor and, as I massaged her tiny heart and breathed gently into her mouth, the tears streamed down my face, wetting hers, I wished with all my heart that I would be able to see her own tears again.

I don't know how much time passed but it felt like an eternity. And just as I was feeling all was lost she gave a tiny shudder and made a hiccupping sound, and vomit started spilling from her mouth. I turned her onto her side so she wouldn't choke and gently put my finger into her mouth to clear it, and as I did so her eyes opened and she looked straight at me.

The commotion had woken Lorie up and she was watching from her cot. I didn't stop to make a phone call - I just gathered them both up, plonked them in the car, grabbed the others, and drove to the hospital.

They were both given the okay but that day I learnt my lesson. It didn't matter how many time the monitors went off, I'd been given a second chance. I never ignored them again.

Chapter Sixteen

FOR BETTER OR FOR WORSE

By the time the twins were born, I felt I was as wedded to my lot in life as I was to my husband. I couldn't have felt luckier to have given birth to my four daughters, but there was still the dull ache of knowing I had truly made my bed now, and that there was no other choice but to lie on it.

I was still living life on a proverbial rollercoaster. Almost all my mental energy focused on the girls; particularly Mirie's reflux, and increasingly, possibly due to exhaustion, unable to see things objectively, certainly as regards my husband. Not that to the outside world we looked like anything other than an ordinary family. Yes, one with their hands full – we had four children, including twin babies – but in all respects just like any other young family. Sometimes stressed, often chaotic, but basically happy.

As we would do, because that was the image Paul always projected to the world. Just as he couldn't countenance the humiliation of his parents finding out he'd lost his driving licence all those years earlier, so the face he presented to the world was one topped by, if not a halo, a shining aura of success. He was a master manipulator and he put his skills to good use; everyone who knew him socially thought he was the most amazing guy on the planet. Only those closest to him – myself, his parents, and our young children, of course – ever got a glimpse of the Paul that existed behind closed doors. Which only served to make me question myself and my feelings, and reinforce my own belief that it must be *me* who was to blame for the troubles we had making our relationship work.

Not that I tried to engage Paul in conversation about his own behaviour any more, because to say anything negative about him – even mild things, such as questioning some small business decision – would always come back to bite me on the bottom. The Paul the world knew was the only Paul in existence, as far as he was concerned. He also told me constantly that *I* was mentally ill and slowly, but surely, I started to wonder if that was the case, despite the mounting evidence to the contrary. As someone who knew him slightly better than most pointed out once, he was his own best PR agent.

And when Paul shone his light on you, you felt it. He could be loving and attentive and was occasionally thoughtfulness personified (usually when he wanted me to get pregnant) and though those times were becoming increasingly rare, they were periods of light and life and laughter that I basked in.

I was also hard-wired to try to make my relationship work and, because it was in my nature to hope for the best, to believe that things might just work out between us. I also had four young lives depending on me, and though I sometimes tried to think how I could achieve sufficient financial independence to make it on my own, in my heart I think I knew the time for flight was over. I knew I would never leave my children, but, feeling so alone in the world, and having not a penny to call my own, I could see no way of leaving *with* them, either. This was true even during the darkest of the dark times; the spectre of giving up, becoming homeless, penniless and haunting the benefits office feeling infinitely more terrifying than staying.

It's a big thing to bear, feeling you are entirely without a loving family, and perhaps that's partly why I couldn't leave Paul. Along with the children we'd created together, Paul now *was* my family. And that knowledge was central to my thinking. They were *our* children, and however difficult Paul was to live with, for all of us, I had made marriage vows now and I meant every one of them. And given my parents' sham of a marriage, I set a lot of store by them, too. That was perhaps why I still had this absolute conviction that I was committed to Paul for life now, for better or for worse, for richer and (increasingly looking likely) for poorer, and that the only way to make that work was to please him. I would do just what his mother had told me I should all those years back – anything I could to try and keep him happy.

And with that conviction came a kind of dogged determination to make the best I could out of what was a steadily worsening situation. Anything I had to do to make life functional and bearable I would do. And, to that end, when Paul's 40th birthday was on the horizon – it was at the beginning of January 1996 - I decided to organise a huge surprise party for him.

And strangely, given everything that had come before it, that party – its conception, its planning and its eventual execution - remains both one of the things I'm most proud of having put together, and an enduring source of some of the few precious happy memories I still have of our lives before Paul's death.

I took to planning Paul's party much as Paul might have done – as a project of supreme importance, which required all the attention and energy I could give it, commencing plans for it almost a whole year before. I booked the same room in the local hotel that had hosted our wedding reception and secretly saved what I could to pay for the best event I could manage. It was organised like a battle campaign; covert and painstaking – with invitations sent out months before, promises of total secrecy elicited, and, in a rare marriage of minds, secret liaisons with his mother, who was naturally very keen to get involved.

His parents also helped financially, by paying for the food, and as he'd decided to take up golf in the months leading up to the big day, I ordered a cake to be made in the shape of a golfing green, and booked a coaching session for him with his dad on the afternoon of the day itself, so that we'd have him out of the way while we decorated the venue.

It was a moment of harmony with Paul's brother, Peter, as well. Peter was two years younger than Paul and by this time had divorced his first wife and was living in London with a lady called Grace. He still had no children of his own but was a natural as an uncle. He wasn't able to visit often but whenever he was due to come, the children couldn't wait to see him. His gifts to them were always thoughtful and he always seemed to enjoy their company, often taking them off for outings and bowling. I often wondered, if he'd had children of his own, what sort of father he might be. A very loving one, I suspected.

His relationship with Paul, however, had become very strained over the years, going back to incidents between them long before we met. He would tell me endlessly about things Peter had done that had upset him from apparently 'overreacting' when Paul touched the arm of a teenage girlfriend, to failing to support him in his musical ambitions and leaving home to pursue his own career. I didn't get involved and I obviously tried to be loyal to my husband but, increasingly, as Paul's paranoia about everything became apparent, I began to see these things in a different light. In any event, I wasn't surprised that Peter had less and less to do with him because although niceties were observed at all times, it was always there, simmering beneath the surface.

Peter was also, I suspect, well aware that Paul was his mother's favourite; he certainly seemed to have spent his youth having to suffer being 'Paul Shanks' brother'. That in itself must have been something of a millstone. Paul was in the school band and something of a school idol – enough to have his name scratched on many girls' desks. And while Peter was a looker in his own right, often being compared to Donny Osmond, he never managed to step out from his older brother's shadow, and certainly lacked his confidence and charisma. No wonder that while Paul stayed with his parents till I prised him away from them, Peter left home and moved away very young.

I think I might have too, because one thing was certain, Paul was his mother's obvious favourite. She always denied it, of course; put it down to birth complications that had made her chronically over-protective, but that neither excused it or changed anything; he was her golden boy and could do no wrong.

But, for tonight, at least, all that family history was forgotten; Peter, ever the gentleman, was my co-conspirator – my 'man on the ground', and was primed to look out for our arrival.

'Where are we off to, then?' Paul asked as we set off for the hotel with Jamie and Kacie and his parents. He knew it was to be a surprise but had no idea what, though his first thought was that we might be going to a concert, as I'd organised a lovely lady from the local church to look after Lorie and Mirie. She babysat for us regularly, adored all the children and, crucially, knew what to do if Mirie had any problems.

Once we turned into the hotel, however, Paul changed his mind. 'We're going for a meal, then?' he suggested. I told him yes.

'Ah, so we're eating in the room we got married in?' he then deduced, working things out as the lift deposited us on the final floor.

'Kind of,' I told him. 'Ah, here's Peter.'

'Oh, is he joining us as well?' he asked. 'That'll be nice.' It had gone like clockwork. He really didn't have a clue.

I watched Peter give the signal as he opened the door on the waiting crowd. Then, as we entered, he pinged the light on and everyone started singing *Happy Birthday*, almost drowned out by the sound of 100 party poppers going off.

The effect was gratifying. Paul stood there, absolutely stunned, as I knew he would be, scanning the room and seeing so many familiar faces grinning back. We'd done well. As well as gathering almost all of his close friends and family, I'd managed to track down all sorts of old friends and colleagues he'd known for years, and from far and wide; even Steve, the friend from way back, who Paul hadn't seen in years and who he'd suggested we have a threesome with back when I'd first met him. Happily, Steve seemed as happy as I was to consign the whole thing to history.

Jamie and Kacie, in particular, had a ball at the party and, seeing them playing, it struck me how valuable their extended family was to them. How badly I wanted that myself; to feel a part of such a big, loving family – to have siblings that felt like friends, cousins, loving aunts and uncles. And having had just the one gran during my child-hood (and, though I was close to her, she wasn't a cuddly one) I longed to feel the warmth of indulgent grandpar-ents in my life. I longed for my children to as well.

I particularly remember how much I enjoyed watch-ing the girls dancing with Paul's dad - their granddad - who, overcoming his natural reticence, had dressed up in a comic Scottish get up (he had Scottish roots) and danced through the crowd making everyone laugh. It was particu-larly poignant, because he *knew* what his son could be like, as did his wife; they had seen his rages often, had been on the *receiving end* of them often, just as I had. How sad it was that they couldn't or wouldn't talk to me, engage with me, to bring about some change in Paul's behaviour. But perhaps they were as wary of upsetting him as I was, and just grateful – the same as I was – to see him happy and smiling, and allowing them to believe that there was really nothing wrong with him. And, for one night only, it felt as though there wasn't.

I had studded the birthday cake with 40 re-igniting candles, and watching Paul's confusion (and everyone's laughter) as he huffed and puffed and tried to blow them out, I remember seeing the happiness on his face and clinging on to that same hope as well. The party, and the memories of it, buoyed me up for weeks – particularly Kacie eating so much of the cake's blue icing that her poo was blue the next morning, and I'd almost rushed her off to hospital before it clicked why.

In fact, I felt so positive about life because of the success of that party, that even when Paul commented a couple of months later that he'd have 'preferred a quiet day with family', I didn't believe him. I'd done the right thing and I felt proud; in fact, I revelled in it. After all, it was a feeling I didn't experience very often.

And perhaps my optimistic, cheery mood was infectious. Paul certainly seemed to sense that I might be receptive to another of his own grand plans, because it wasn't long after his birthday when he began badgering me again about having another baby. It was in early summer, after our accountant Richard's own 40th bash in London, which had been a grand affair held in an enormous marquee.

We'd returned home it was on one of those wonderful June evenings when it was warm enough to sit out and eat on the patio, and light enough to stay out quite late. Having waved off the babysitter, we'd brought everything outside; the homemade dining table, the chairs and the twins' and Kacie's highchairs, and prepared a meal – coincidentally one of Paul's favourite tortellini dishes, with cream and tomato sauce, which the girls loved as well.

'You know what?' he said. 'I've been thinking. I feel we're not all here yet.' He grinned at me. 'I think we should try for another baby.'

I stopped mid-mouthful, gobsmacked. What was he *talking* about? The children, of course, couldn't have been more excited.

Chapter Seventeen

TANTRUMS AND TIARAS

They were little girls, of course. They *would* be excited. But I really couldn't fathom it. We were struggling financially, we had four small, demanding daughters and, what with Mirie's reflux issues and some of Lorie's more difficult behaviours, I was already beginning to feel that they might be slightly more demanding than most. It would be a while before the truth dawned and we began getting the diagnoses that would begin to explain their various difficulties, but it just felt ridiculous to bring another life into a family that was already under so much strain. But Paul was ridiculously, puppyishly, excited by the idea, and kept citing his aunt as an example of what he had in mind. She had raised nine children, after all – and it had all worked out fine. Wouldn't it be great if our children's childhoods could be like theirs?

But by this time, I knew Paul's real motivation was slightly different. An unguarded comment one day made that very clear. There were a local couple we knew called Guy and Cathy, who already had six children, and who seemed to manage their brood very well. 'Wouldn't it be great if we could beat them?' Paul commented one day.

Said by someone else, this might have just seemed a jokey aside. But I knew better. Paul was serious, even though it still made no sense to me. He was obsessed with controlling his environment, after all, and kids always created the exact opposite. Couldn't he already *see* that? It seemed to me that it was more about amassing trophies than anything. He certainly didn't seem to want to do much parenting. His idea of childrearing seemed mostly to involve making containment structures out of plywood.

He seemed to like to 'corral' the children, generally. Because we could no longer afford to send the girls to nursery, and we were both working, he decided to fit gates to every door on the house and keep them contained in one room out of the way. I found this unbearable to cope with – what mother wouldn't? – so his solution was to build an office area in the one room they were allowed in, but with a fence all around it so they could see me but not get to me, rather as he'd created the playpen for Jamie when she was small. As any parent would understand, that just made everything so much worse. It was torture for them, as toddlers, not to be able to actually interact with me when I was right there. And, of course, I couldn't concentrate. It was the worse 'solution' ever, in terms of doing work.

But work we must – even if it was for someone else, and for less money, because we needed to keep a roof over our heads. And things were dire – though Paul still went on endless seminars trying to make a go of Amway, we'd by now had to enter into an IVA (Individual Voluntary Arrangement: one step down from bankruptcy) and had a strict repayment programme for all the banks and other organisations we owed money to, so every single penny counted. While Paul was dreaming about siring a football team, I would be scrabbling around for loose change to buy milk.

Even so, Paul seemed to live in a kind of parallel universe in which the harsh realities of like had no place; he had started life a dreamer and perhaps he always would be. Though he no longer played and sang for money, his love of music had never waned and though he was proficient on a guitar, his real desire was to play the piano. He'd spent his adult life hell-bent on learning it, too – though never to the extent that he actually could. He'd constantly start lessons but would give them up every time; as if even his inability to get to grips with it was a conspiracy in itself.

He still wrote songs, too – and wrote a special one for each of his children as they came into the world, and one cherished memory they have is of having 'their' song sung to them. He was also determined that his children should be musical themselves – never mind whether they had any natural aptitude. To that end, Jamie had piano lessons for a couple of years, followed by Kacie, who lasted less than half as long. He decided they should have a piano each, as well, so we ended up with two – a number that swelled to *five*, which I still struggle to believe – which were dotted around the house, and as he eventually turned much of the downstairs into an open plan space, if one was playing it was impossible for another one to play at the same time as the noise carried all too well.

He also gradually bought all the children guitars, so we ended up with seven or eight of them as well, even though not one had the slightest interest in learning, and their musical talent – mostly for singing, as with their father – would only be evident years down the line.

Paul would also enthuse endlessly – to the older two, particularly – about all the grand plans he had for them, too. About how one day soon we'd all be off to Disneyland, and how he'd take them to the 'Diamond Ball' (an Amway incentive, for people who 'went Diamond' in terms of sales) in gilt carriages, wearing beautiful designer dresses, the envy of all. One of many promises to the children he seemed to derive such pleasure from making. It was just so desperately sad that not one of them came true.

CHAPTER EIGHTEEN

'WE'RE NOT ALL HERE YET'

By now, Paul's new favourite expression of 'we're not all here yet' had become a kind of mantra by which we lived our lives, and within the following four years, I had three further children. Another pattern had developed now; though I couldn't see it then. I would live day to day, soldiering on, trying to second-guess Paul's rants and mood-swings, and then, one day, everything would change in our relationship. The 'other', loving, attentive Paul would move back in with us, telling me how much he loved me, often several times a day, and for however long it took to cajole me into having another child, launch a general charm offensive that ensnared me in its seductive web. And it seemed that I was powerless to resist him. Feeling so tied to him, and so unloved for so much of the time, that feeling of *being* loved was something like a drug to me, my need for it eclipsing all rational thought. It's hard to over-emphasise how much that feeling of being desired and cherished meant to me. I had lived my whole childhood with an undemonstrative, emotionally absent mother, and a cold, dictatorial father, and had never experienced any kind of romantic relationship as an adult where another person's love felt only as much as I deserved.

So I was stupidly grateful every time I experienced it, and would, ironically, rationalise away all rational thought. Perhaps this time, I'd always think, because at this point I still loved him, the change in my husband would last. Perhaps he was mellowing in his 'old' age. Perhaps maturing. I couldn't see the reality - that him getting me to create children was like any other grand plan for him. A military exercise, approached coldly and forensically. But that's what it was – another project. As soon as I fell pregnant, that 'other' loving Paul would disappear.

But the proverbial rollercoaster that was my relationship with Paul was contrasted by the thrill of finding that motherhood suited me so well. That thing that I never expected to fulfil me was doing just that - giving me so, so much more than I could have imagined. Much to my surprise I thoroughly enjoyed being a mum and absolutely adored mothering my four children. I loved watching them play and I revelled in all their antics, which were often bizarre as they were all still under five. I loved the process of feeding them healthy food and taking care of them generally – something I never expected but to my surprise and delight, seemed to satisfy a very deep need in me.

Jamie was a bright, lively child who was difficult to handle and there was no doubt she could be very defiant. But when she walked into a room it was like the sun coming out. Kacie was mischievous and constantly smiling. She also had a 'knowing' look in her eye; everyone agreed it made her look as though she'd been here before. Mirie spent her entire life laughing. She was a giggler; anything could set her off and it seemed most things did. She was a delightful toddler - always up to something funny and engaging and she and Lorie were so close it was almost supernatural.

Lorie was the only one that concerned me. She'd changed from being a very easy baby – one who rarely demanded attention – into a toddler who was now very high maintenance due to her ever more worrying challenges. She'd become a fussy eater and needed the constant reassurance of the film 'Free Willy' playing, especially at meal times. She would shut down or scream for no apparent reason, and a little warning bell that all was not quite as it should be was beginning to sound intermittently in my head.

On the business front, however, things were steadily improving. In what felt like a rare moment of sharp business acumen, Paul had come up with the idea for starting another business; one similar to the Classic Casinos business we'd sold, but different – it was to be called Big Indoor Games. Its beauty lay in the fact that unlike Classic Casinos, it would do fewer casinos and more games, so wouldn't require the recruitment of so many specialist croupier staff – a big bonus as they were hard to find. It would also have broader appeal due to being more diverse; we'd do all sorts of different games, only bigger.

Paul was building again, too – something that always made him happy – and with the experience of the previous equipment he was making everything much lighter, meaning it would be much less onerous to store and transport. We also knew that, if we worked hard, we'd be able to drum up plenty of business, both from new clients after something a little bit different from the usual casino, and from old clients who trusted us to deliver.

It was an incredibly intense time, getting our new business show on the road, so when our fifth daughter was born in 1997, I felt shattered – something I perhaps should have got used to by now. Once again the pregnancy was not without incident, my body having its own views, as ever, as to when I should be having the baby, and requiring a hospital stay to fend her off at 28 weeks.

But she was safely delivered, at the right time, in June, leading us quickly on to the other now reliable complication of what to call her. Here, for once, I managed to score a small victory. Paul wanted to call her Nikie (this one had to start with a N, of course), but that felt way too much like Vikie to me, and my suggestion of Nikita (having listened to the Elton John song) was dismissed as both having too many letters and not ending in 'ie'. But I put my foot down, and, for once, Paul conceded defeat without a fight. As long as the second name was only four letters, so we'd still end up with ten) and ended with an 'a' to match Nikita, I could have it. Which made it easy. Her second name would be Nina.

My own 40th birthday came around in February 1998, and it's a foolish woman who doesn't learn from experience, so I had little in the way of expectations. Even so, even my modest hopes weren't to be satisfied. I spent the morning in the hairdressers, having my hair cut and styled; an appointment

I had obviously organised myself. And later that day, Paul presented me with a plate of jam tarts, on which my name had been spelt out in icing, each tart bearing a candle – though not, in this case, of the re-igniting kind.

That said, Paul did make something of an effort that evening, taking me to Pizza Express for a meal while a babysitter looked after the children, during which we had a really long, positive chat about the future. It was at times like those that I believed we had one – and a good one, at that – so if I recall my 40th it's always with that uppermost in my mind; that it was a day filled with hope.

Nikita was only nine months old when I found out I was expecting another baby, and despite the relative sunniness of my then outlook, and the prospects for our growing family, I found myself struck down with guilt. It was a new guilt as well; guilt about the population of the planet - we were nearly in the 21st century after all and with five children under seven and another on the way, it felt more than reckless; it seemed almost morally unsound. Paul couldn't have been happier – he was well on the way to beating the neighbours, but I felt ashamed at bringing so many children in the world; in tandem with our precarious financial situation, I felt I couldn't really justify it to anyone.

I consoled myself, often, with one inalienable fact. Paul and I had three brothers between us who had not produced children, and now never would, so if disapproval came my way and I needed to fight my corner, I as least had that riposte up my sleeve. And a part of me (a small but important part) didn't care. I'd never cared what gender my babies were when I was carrying them; it was one reason I never asked to know. But as soon as I had my boy I cherished him. Osborn-Oran (as Paul soon named him, to match the rule for Nikita-Nina) felt like a gift. Even if our gift to him – to grow up with five older sisters – felt as if it might be something of a poisoned chalice…

But we weren't done yet. Just before Christmas 2000, I gave birth to another daughter. I had lost my father that August, almost half way through the pregnancy, and we now saw so little of one another that he didn't even know. He'd been ill for a while so it wasn't entirely unexpected, and seeing his body before the funeral felt very strange. Whilst Brenda sobbed and held his hand, wailing that she couldn't believe he was gone, and how much she loved him and would miss him, all I could think was "What was all that about?"

The way he had conducted himself in life meant he had no friends. Though a few people respected his ability as an engineer, everyone who knew him was scared of him and no one liked him as a person. His funeral reflected this - the only attendees were myself, Paul, Brenda, Tony and two of his old colleagues from work.

His passing barely touched me, except as a reminder of just how blessed I was to have my children, and how passionate was my love for them all. And now I had seven – a final daughter, who was called Pippa-Peita: In her case I was keen to revert to the first naming rule. I was happy to keep to the alphabet rule, too, as I was keen to call her Pippa, because it was a name I had always loved, and that of the daughter of my long term friend, the dentist in

London I'd known since I was 17. The 'Pieta' was a version of Paul's brother's name, Peter.

It was a Christmas that I'll always remember. As with the previous two pregnancies, I spent time as a hospital in-patient before Pippa's birth, and was forever backwards and forwards between the maternity and labour wards and constantly in pain with contractions. So it was a relief that she was born four weeks early, like most of the others, and even more so that she weighed a very respectable 7lbs.

But our problems had only just started. Within a couple of days she developed Jaundice, and though I wasn't unduly worried – four of the others had been jaundiced when born - it did mean a regime of keeping her in hospital and under lights till her bilirubin levels were acceptable. It being so close to Christmas, however, the hospital were keen to get us home (I stayed in with her) and we were discharged on the 22nd on strict instruction that I continue to breastfeed, which I was keen to do anyway, and that we 'park' her by the patio doors during the daytime to benefit from maximum daylight.

The children were naturally ecstatic that they'd have the new baby home for Christmas, but the excitement was destined to be short-lived. Only the following day, while Paul's brother Peter and his then partner Lorraine were up for a Christmas visit, the midwife arrived for her own daily visit and announced that she wasn't happy with Pippa's colour. She took some blood and hurried off, saying she'd be back as soon as possible, only to return within the hour with the frightening news that her bilirubin had shot up to a dangerous level, and she had to be returned to the special care unit NOW!

We were off like a shot, me yelling apologies over my shoulder as I hurried after her, and once again Pippa was stripped off and back under lights, the prospect of her being home for Christmas looking unlikely after all. There were now only two days to go and I spent them on the hoof, rushing backwards and forwards to the hospital to give her those precious breastfeeds, and while at home, expressing milk using the pump the hospital had given me so that I wouldn't have to do the overnight ones as well.

There was also the small matter of Christmas shopping. Having been in hospital for most of the final weeks of the pregnancy, I'd hardly had a chance to do any at all. So, between feeds, I hot-footed it off to buy presents for the children and pull together some semblance of a celebration.

Paul's parents had come up for Christmas as always and because I'd expressed sufficient milk the afternoon before, I was able to prepare lunch, along with Paul's mother, and to sit down and eat it, at least. I then left everyone to clear away and drove to the hospital to see how Pippa was doing and to give her a feed. When I got there the staff were overjoyed to be able to tell me that it would be safe to take her home. No one was expecting it, including me, so it would be a lovely surprise when I returned home with her.

It's at time such as those that it hits you most forcefully what the idea of family really means. When I walked in, Pippa tucked into her baby car seat beside me, the response from the children was overwhelming. They didn't care about their Christmas presents: having Pippa home *was* their Christmas present, and they were falling over each other in their haste to be the first to be allowed to sit and hold her. I remember that moment well. No, her jaundice probably hadn't been life-threatening, and had she had to stay in longer, it wouldn't have been the end of the world – Christmas is, after all, just another day. But she felt like a gift, our 'Millennium' baby, and as I sat among the children, shattered, I was content to just observe them. Content in the knowledge that whatever life brought them, these seven children were bonded for life.

A new life takes its toll on a mother, physically and men-tally, and once the festive flush of wellbeing was replaced by the daily grind, things began to settle back into a more familiar pattern – the sheer grind that was looking after so many children.

The previous autumn had been a record year for rain-fall, with extensive flooding, and the spring was shaping up to be similarly sodden, making everything to do with little ones so much more difficult. So, for a period, as the mother of seven kids I never thought I'd have, I was com-pletely shell-shocked and exhausted. I had had a decade of either being pregnant or breastfeeding – sometimes both! – and was weighed down by the guilt of knowing it had all been self-inflicted. I would sit and ponder, particu-larly in the early, foggy weeks before the coming of spring, and wonder how my life had turned out to be so different from the one I'd envisaged when, as a young independent woman, free of the shackles of my troubled childhood, I'd daydream about the exciting life I might lead.

I wasn't after sympathy – I didn't want any and I cer-tainly knew I didn't deserve any – but as I trudged through those early days, it was only the sense of responsibility for my children that got me through. Paul had got his way; we had 'beaten' the neighbours, if not quite his auntie.

But how to put into words how much I loved my children? Perhaps no mother can. All I knew was that they completed me. They gave me a huge sense of self-worth where previously I had had none, and I wanted to be the best mother I possibly could to them. I adored every one of them and cuddling them and being cuddled back was, to my mind, the best feeling in the world.

My family complete – *whatever* Paul said, though thankfully, he no longer nagged about it – I realised that far from shy away from it, I now relished my immersion in motherhood. I was a driven woman now; excited at the prospect of giving my brood the kind of childhood I'd never had. A childhood full of warmth and love and physical affection; something I'd craved so much as a child myself, and which seemed to come so naturally to me as a mum. Despite the challenges life with Paul involved, I felt energised because of them; loved watching them grow and change and develop, facing the various hurdles they all had to jump.

It was the beginning of a process that would become lifelong; educating myself about their various needs and devoting myself to their care, and there was no doubt that my concerns about 'normality' had now subtly shifted focus. Due to Paul's personality traits and mental health issues, our lives *were* abnormal, and in a myriad different ways, but there were new challenges to be overcome now. I was becoming increasingly concerned about whether all our children were coping – not just from the vagaries of our odd, increasingly difficult lifestyle, but with what was going on inside *them.*

Lorie's development, in particular, was worrying me. Both twins had delayed speech and had already been referred to a speech and language therapist. And while Mirie's were soon attributed to problems with her hearing, Lorie's weren't, and was looking increasingly likely that their origin was very different; that she might be on the autistic spectrum.

While we were in the process of getting her seen by the right people and, if appropriate, formally diagnosed, Osborn, too, seemed to be wrestling with challenges. In his case, not only with potential autism – which was also looking likely - but with his balance, which was extremely poor, and which I struggled to make sense of, as no one seemed to be able to get to the root of.

But while the challenges with my young children took up much of my time, there was the ever-present spectre of their father's eccentricities, which were increasingly looking far less like benign quirks of nature, and a great deal more indicative of a truly fractured mind. Even as I was shedding welcome light on the children's individual challenges, the storm clouds were gathering up ahead.

CHAPTER NINETEEN
HOME SWEET HOME

March 2001

In the spring of the year following Pippa's birth, Paul decided that the children and I should move out of the house temporarily, his idea being that with us out of the way, he could work at building our games business, Big Indoor Games, more efficiently, and also do some work on the kitchen.

I had no problem with either of these developments, to be fair. Though Paul still had plans with Amway, his enthusiasm and energy were fading, and I was much more confident we could make a go of another games business. I was also keen to make improvements to our kitchen. Catering for a family as large as ours was always going to be a challenge, and, given that Paul's parents still spent so many weekends staying with us, there were often eleven of us sitting down for meals. I would cook in saucepans the size of cauldrons, reminiscent of what you'd see in a restaurant kitchen, and was developing muscles that Popeye himself would have been proud of. One of Paul's plans, therefore, was to replace our standard cooker with an enormous range, which would give us the capacity we so badly required.

But to move out and pay rent, when we were already paying a terrifying mortgage? To me, that was insane. And I knew that his need to change things was every bit as much about his obsession with creating the strange living environment that he seemed to need. He had done so much to the house already in his quest for minimalism, all without planning permission and much of it potentially dangerous, to my mind.

He'd also cleared out almost all the living spaces. As well as getting us down to just a couple of sticks of furniture (the children's bedrooms now contained no furniture at all now, bar a bed or mattress) he'd also removed several supporting walls. But, as usual, he could not be dissuaded from the project. Despite my pleading with him not to, he had already re-mortgaged the house, and when I wanted to know how this new kitchen would be funded, finally admitted he'd also borrowed money from a 'friend' several months before.

This was seriously worrying news. The 'friend', though indeed an old friend from Paul's school days with whom he'd kept in touch, turned out to be a loan shark, and finding out Paul had borrowed money that I knew we couldn't afford was extremely worrying. Worse than that, however, was finding out – because he could find no way to bury it – was that the £2000 we were paying out every quarter wasn't even paying anything off. It was interest – set at 10% per quarter.

It was extremely hard to find a place big enough and close enough to suit our needs, but we eventually settled on a four bedroom bungalow about ten miles from home, which though compact, with only one lounge/diner as living space, at least had a garage that could be used for an office, though it was far from ideal for a family of nine. It was then a case of dismantling beds and packing as much as was practical to take with us, then, over a period of several days, going backwards and forwards with the company van, children and I duly moving in.

Once we were in, however, I began to see positives. Being away from Paul during the day was one, and it was a big one. At least I could live the way the majority of people did i.e. not being with their partner 24/7. I knew I would be far more productive in the office – even with a toddler on my hands – than I could ever be when Paul was around, hovering over me, needing me to do the things he couldn't face doing himself. This in turn meant that, come the evenings, I could take off my work hat and actually spend time with my children.

But my initial optimism was soon to be drummed out of me, because it became clear that this wasn't going to happen. Almost every day, Paul would find reasons why I needed to be back at the house; doing some 'important' clerical job or other (that could apparently only be done there) or to offer an opinion about some detail of the kitchen remodelling or other and generally offer praise for his efforts. Most weekdays, therefore, after taking the older children to their various schools and Osborn to his nursery, Pippa and I would have to make the ten mile journey back home, spend most of the day there, with me alternately having to do admin that I could just as easily do from the bungalow or, more often, having to sit and hear about some perceived slight or other, or some terrible 'conspiracy' the bank or some client or other had cooked up.

It was a very curious version of 'being a family'. Though initially Paul would return to the bungalow every night, it soon became the norm that he would only return at weekends and for the occasional night. And when Paul did deign to spend any time with us, tensions ran high and, with the upheaval of moving and the children's various issues, it was a struggle to get through every day. It was also financial lunacy. Paul had always managed the money side of the business, but I knew how we were doing, and, increasingly, the income we were generating through Big Indoor Games wasn't stacking up against the money we actually had. Not to mention shelling out: We were paying £1000 per month to live on top of each other in cramped accommodation, while we had a home of our own ten miles down the road – one we were already paying a fortune in mortgage repayments on. So it was no wonder that, as the weeks dragged on and on, things were bound to boil over.

Though, ironically, it was to be something of a useful wake-up call for me. By now, I was beginning to take stock of my little brood, and was becoming increasingly alert to the possibility that at least a couple of them might have special needs. Lorie had been formally diagnosed as having an Autistic Spectrum Disorder back in 1999, when she'd been four, though I (and the doctors) had informally known that for longer. I'd also long had my concerns that Jamie might be slightly autistic too, though as her behaviours manifested themselves in markedly different ways from Lorie, it wasn't something anyone could really put their finger on.

Kacie, on the other hand, seemed to be thriving and developing normally – though it didn't escape my notice that, given my family background, I had little instinctive idea of what 'developing normally' might mean.

I was certainly still concerned about Osborn. He'd had mobility issues almost as soon as he was able to move around and had been almost two years old before he could even pull himself up to standing. Even then, when letting go, he'd often fall over. And when he did start to walk he was very unsteady on his feet, the slightest touch often causing him to topple over. He also struggled to use crayons and eating implements, and was generally very uncoordinated, all of which was becoming a real worry. And though Pippa was still so young, I was anxious about her as well because she was also consistently failing to hit her development milestones.

All of this added up to the move causing an added headache because it just added to the hours spent to-ing and fro-ing to get the children to heir various health checks. It was Nikita, however, who was worrying me the most now, because at three and a half she had so little language that she was virtually silent, and, as a consequence, seemed locked in her own little world. Was she autistic? Even more so than Lorie?

Some of the things she did certainly seemed to suggest she might be. In recent months, for example, she'd developed a habit of spitting all the time, regardless of where she was. She'd do it when she was out and about, causing strangers to stare at her, and also at home. She would spit wherever she was in the house, which naturally included the living room carpet. Being so young, she didn't understand that wasn't socially acceptable, and I was having a devil of a time trying to break the habit, as were her nursery, who'd also flagged it up. The trouble was that we were at a loss to know why she was doing it, as was to become the case so often over the coming years. As it was, my then 'strategy' was to supply her with tissues for nursery and at least have her spit into those.

One Saturday night we were all at the bungalow, Paul having made one of his regular weekend visits, when, without warning, Nikita spat on the carpet. We'd been sitting watching TV (me being vigilant with my ever-present loo roll) but though I'd become quite adept at doing ninja leaps to catch what she produced, on this occasion she was sitting on the floor, cross-legged, and spat on the floor between them before could get to her.

Paul lost the plot completely. 'Stop that!' he yelled at her, causing her to burst into tears. 'That's disgusting! You're a very naughty girl!

Nikita naturally became very distressed but because she had so little language at her disposal, her response when feeling vulnerable was either to scream or shut down. She did both, which only angered Paul more.

'She doesn't mean to do it!' I tried, though he totally ignored me.

'Da-ad!' joined in Kacie and Jamie, distressed too. 'Stop it! She doesn't mean it! Stop shouting at her!'

But it was like whispering in the wind for all the notice Paul took of us.

In fact, the more we tried to stop him shouting, the angrier Paul seemed to get – a pattern familiar to us all. Soon he was shouting a stream of abuse at her and, as ever, Nikita responded in the only way she could - shutting down and looking at the floor.

'She can't answer you!' I kept telling him. 'So why do you keep asking her why she does it? It's not that she won't, it's that she can't!'

He ignored me again, pointing his finger in her face and shaking her, and the more he yelled, the more she became locked inside herself – I could see her retreating from him with every blast of furious shouting, unable to communicate at all.

He picked her up finally, about an hour after he'd first begun his tirade; an hour in which, after my initial attempts to calm things, the other children, taking my lead, had kept trying to reason with their father as well. No more; he clearly wanted her alone. She screamed as he picked her up and when I leapt instinctively to try and pull her away from him, held her even more tightly and stomped out of the bungalow with her. We could only watch, traumatised, as he took her to his car and then sat there, continuing to shout at her – we could still hear him from indoors – while she sat, mute and scared, in the passenger seat.

The whole process of Paul trying to stop Nikita spitting took three hours to play out. Three long hours before he eventually gave up and brought her in again, pale and exhausted, at 11pm. It did no good. It was five years before she finally grew out of it.

Years later Nikita *was* able to articulate the reason. She was able to tell me that the reason she spat was because she always thought she had a fly in her mouth. Apparently she'd been outside one day when she was little and one had flown into her mouth and from then on, for all that time, having not seen it fly out again, she'd still believed it was there.

Most people make the best of it when having new kitchens fitted, because, for most, the whole process takes a few weeks at most. Not so for us; with much of our once beautiful home having been turned into a virtual building site, the process of making it liveable again took ten long months. We returned to the house just before Christmas, some £30,000 further in debt.

CHAPTER TWENTY
UNRAVELLED

With seven children, life was never going to be normal again, and as the months passed and Pippa grew out of the exhausting baby stage, I began to be ambushed by unexpected moments of pure joy; catching them laughing together, immersed in some complicated game, being kind to one another, relating to each other – and I'd be taken aback at just how blessed I felt to have them.

But even by the time we had a clearer idea of the various challenges they'd be facing (Osborn and Pippa's Cerebral Palsy, and the varying degrees of Autistic Spectrum Disorder present in the rest) it was Paul's behaviour that was proving the most vexatious. Increasingly worrying was just how much stranger it was becoming. To me, at any rate. To the children he was behaving as he always had i.e. being predictably unpredictable. They had known no other life than the one they'd been born into so their often aggressive, always bullying, sometimes absent, but almost always frightening father, was just doing more of the same.

Life was, as ever, all about Paul being able to control everything, which meant the constant introduction of new 'regimes' to achieve this. These could change without warning, and regularly did. On any given week the children could expect something different. For some time he made me keep out of the house (I would trail them round a shop called Big W, in Coventry, and give them tea there) and we would not be allowed home till I called and was given permission. Sometimes I'd call and be told it was too early and to stay out longer - sometimes way beyond the younger children's bedtimes. I would defy him on occasion, especially when it started compromising the children's health and wellbeing, but I would pay the price – an inevitable violent row, which only served to compromise their emotional health.

Some regimes did make sense – coming home and doing homework en masse being one of them – but most were draconian and silly; more a worrying example of the entrenched nature of his obsessive compulsive tendencies than anything else. One particular one involved the children being made to dress for school all together downstairs. They would then have to place their pyjamas in perfect piles around the dining table and then, when they returned from school, immediately reverse the whole process, undressing under his supervision as soon as they were home and leaving their school clothes in neat piles instead. Even the youngest ones hated the lack of privacy and the humiliation, so there was much relief when this particular 'regime' was scrapped.

We were made to leave the house at weekends, too – all day Saturday and Sunday – and, for a time, armed with our season tickets and a basic picnic, we would haunt Drayton Manor theme park relentlessly. I think my children must be in the tiniest minority imaginable – greeting the words 'Drayton Manor' with groans instead of cheers.

Paul also put them to work. He would dream up ridiculously grand but pointless schemes, rather as he did chasing his business dreams, and many days, particularly during the summer holidays, would see all the children press-ganged into becoming a team of unpaid labourers. On one occasion, having cleared the field of topsoil ready to plant new grass seed, he had them form a chain of human buckets over a two day period before and after school, just to remove larger stones and stray bits of metal and plastic. Fair enough – it's good for children to do chores around the house and garden – but this was 10 or 11 acres, and it really wasn't funny.

Another time he had them sorting pens and pencils. If you have experience of, or suffered from, Obsessive Compulsive Disorder, you will probably be familiar with the various – and sometimes bizarre – ways it manifests itself in a person. And perhaps, had I understood what the term OCD meant then, I would have seen Paul's behaviours in a different, more medical light. As it was, he had no sense that he had any psychological problems. It was the world that had things wrong, not him.

I often wonder, looking back, how different things might have been, had I come from a cohesive happy family. I'll never know – and I'll obviously never regret having my seven beautiful children – but I wonder if, in some way, our relationship was predestined from the start; if the reason we stayed together was precisely because that, in me, Paul had found someone who not only lacked that vital strength-giving security (which might have enabled me to leave him early on), but who had no yardstick with which to measure 'normal'. And that *was* me. I'd had a strange, loveless, isolated childhood. I lost my mother early on, and of all the essentials I lacked growing up perhaps the most damaging in terms of my relationship choices was that I had no real concept of what constituted 'normal' behaviour.

I was equally isolated from the 'normal' world now. Paul was charismatic; a consummate professional with charm and smoke and mirrors, and, just as is so often the case with privately abused women, the public face of the Shanks family was a smiling one. But it was a mask; I was in a relationship with a *far* from normal man. And the irony is that I had by now got a yardstick; one that normalised behaviours that displayed a profoundly abnormal mind. So much so that I had long since ceased to see just how odd his behaviours were, in that I would put them down to Paul just 'being Paul'.

For the children, it was perhaps even worse. A child adapts to their surroundings; that's what they are hard-wired to do. And Paul's world was the only one they'd ever known. So it didn't much matter how bizarre were the tasks and projects he would get them to do, they would simply accept it and do them. Yes, they were grudging about it sometimes – what child isn't? - and as they got older and more aware of how friends lived, they must have wondered at the strange world they inhabited at home, but they were far too scared of their father's wrath to question it.

One of Paul's most entrenched behaviours was that of maintaining his precious diaries. He'd kept one and updated it daily for almost all of his life; usually a big hardback A4 double-page-per-day one, with narrow feint and margin. One of his annual rituals latterly was to take a ruler and divide each page further, so he could categorise his activities, plans and thoughts – which he would then enter, in his incredibly tiny writing.

This habit had now taken on a new level of obsessiveness. He'd become more secretive about them, guarding them jealously, and writing ever more detailed accounts. And on the odd occasion I got a glimpse of them, it was into a world that confounded me. As well as detailing his days and meetings to the minutest degree, he would also record everything he ate, everyone he spoke to – however fleeting and unimportant the encounter – and precisely time every single phone conversation, even the ten minute chats about nothing he regularly had with his mother. There also seemed to be a system of highlighting in place; whole areas were highlighted, neat to a fault, though for what reason I couldn't begin to guess.

He applied the same sort of logic to material things. He had become a hoarder; he would never throw *anything* away. The perhaps 'acceptable' manifestation of this took the shape of the children's clothing, which now occupied a partitioned off room, with a long hanging rail and various boxes, which took up one whole wall of our now cavernous single downstairs living space. He would have me trawl the charity shops and various clothing sales to clothe the children and, of course, we did a great line in passing everything down. But nothing – not a thing – could he part with. When the hoard became overwhelming he'd never consider giving stuff back to charity or sending things to be recycled – he'd simply box it and store it somewhere else; usually the enormous barn at the back of the house.

And it wasn't just clothing. He would sort and store everything, no matter how seemingly insignificant. He would keep every single toy ever included in a cereal packet, every Christmas stocking filler, every broken plaything, every eraser and damaged kitchen gadget – he'd even keep scraps of paper with unintelligible scribble on them, and the broken parts that had come off the broken toys. All were sorted separately, all were carefully labelled, all quickly whisked away to storage.

It would be years before the staggering extent of this compulsion hit home to me, and I had an answer to the mystery of all the household items that would inexplicably disappear. But in the meantime, sorting and re-sorting was often the order of the day, usually for boxes of ancient tat that belonged in the rubbish. And so it was with his huge collection of pens and pencils, which, one beautiful summer morning, he decided had to be sorted out. It was 6am when he got the children up, and this was nothing unusual. When he'd decided upon a project there was no question of anyone having a lie-in.

They were presented with several large boxes of pens, pencils and felt-tipped that Paul had accumulated – and, of course, kept – over many years. There were thousands of them, literally, and these were not the children's either. This was in addition to their own, though if they left any lying about, woe betide them – they would join Paul's collection too; a collection they were not allowed to touch under any circumstances - other than this one, of course.

Once the children were assembled, Paul explained that they would sort the boxes out in several stages. First they must test every pen to see if it was working, and these would go into a box which he would test himself later. Next they had to sort the remainder by type – be they pen, pencil, felt tip or crayon. That done, and the items in separate boxes, they had to sort each category of writing implement into colours, and woe betide them if they got any of them wrong.

They usually did; perhaps putting a greeny-blue pen into the 'blue' box. And then he would shout at the culprit, loudly. It was the same with every ambiguous colour. Finally, the job completed, they would be allowed to go and play and the new set of boxes, neatly labelled, would be returned straight to storage. Again, this would be in the barn, or, increasingly now, to one of the storage units in Harbury that he had been renting for several years – a distance of about 10 miles by road.

While Paul was collecting all this clutter, the house itself had become virtually empty. When we'd bought Birches Wood Farm, back in 1986, it had been a beautiful family home. Now the house itself was little more than a shell. Our cold, cavernous living space, the result of him demolishing various internal walls, contained only a couple of settees, a few armchairs, a home-made dining table and a TV, and that was pretty much it. Even the television cabinet my father had bought us as a wedding present had – inexplicably – disappeared now. Without being able to supply a reason other than muttering that it was getting too 'tatty', Paul had one day decided it had to go. He'd done it when I was out with all the children – as I so often was – and rather than consign it to incarceration in a storage unit, he'd already burned it before I arrived home.

Paul's quest for minimalism extended to the children's rooms as well. Each had a bed (if they were lucky) or just a mattress on the floor. None had a proper wardrobe or chest of drawers for their clothes; with the clothing store downstairs (large enough to fill at least a couple of charity shops) they were allowed just a cheap hanging rail from Argos and a cardboard box for anything that couldn't be hung from it. They would often return home from going to tea at various friends' houses and marvel wide-eyed at the poshness of their bedrooms, prompting me, one day, in a rare fit of defiance, to buy them all one of those cheap open towers, which had spaces for all their sock and pants. That this was such a major thing probably says it all.

Even with my desensitisation over 15-odd years, by any yardstick you cared to use, by the early 2000s the accumulation of my husband's odd behaviours was reaching unacceptable and terrifying levels. Paul was becoming more volatile, antagonistic, secretive, obsessive and just downright peculiar by the year. But the more I tried to gently suggest that he perhaps needed some sort of help, the more explosive and terrifying was his fury. 'You're the one who's mentally ill!' he'd rage and rage at me, almost hysterically. It was the same thing he'd always done; caused me to question myself wretchedly, but now I knew differently, and had plenty of evidence to prove it. All I needed now was for someone else on the outside to see it too.

In that regard, Paul had managed to keep things well hidden. Hardly anyone but his parents and the guys that worked for us ever came to the house and the only one to raise concerns so far had been Sally Jones, the children's nursery school teacher, but not so much that I could marshall her and take action. But with my concern escalating, I now tried to broach the reality of his behaviour with his parents – something I'd previously decided there was no point in doing. Surely, by now, they too could see how their son had changed? Surely they were worried about his extremes of mood? His manic scheming? His mental health? But their response was as it had even been – he was just stressed. As if 'stress' was the magic word that explained and excused everything. As if using the word 'stress' was almost like a charm, which opened an aperture in the sand for them to bury their heads in.

I enjoyed no such luxury. And I had to remember that I had witnessed the way Paul could terrorise his parents first-hand many times over the years. But it was happening even so, and I needed to act; the fact that Paul was unravelling mentally was no longer something I could talk myself out of, and, in a strange way, a part of me clung hopefully to the fact that what he'd previously been so adept at hiding from the world at large, was spilling out sufficiently that it was beginning to be noticed – if not by his parents, by *someone* at least.

People were certainly beginning to pass comment. As my friend Ingrid observed one day, surprising me with her perceptiveness, I would never know, when I returned home from going out, if he'd 'be tap dancing on the table or have his head in the oven'. Such was the reality of living with such a fractured mind. And I knew he felt tortured, too. Though it was impossible to get through to him that there might be other reasons why he felt the whole world was out to get him; reasons related to what was going on in his head. It was hopeless; the minute I tried to make any suggestion of that nature, he just shut down, telling me, as he always did, that it was *me* who was insane.

Paul had taken to sneaking around, as well. I was by now well used to his regular 'absenteeism' as I'd come to think of it; the engineering of work commitments that enabled him to duck out of family life, often for days at a time. I was also used to his selectivity about whom he would and wouldn't speak to. For a time he had a like-minded friend called Jim (a man who also worked from us from time to time and who shared Paul's OCD – Jim suffers from it severely) and if he called round, Paul would appear like magic, as if from nowhere, and suddenly become this smiling and energetic 'fun dad', much to the bemusement of the children. This would go on for precisely the length of Jim's visits, then he would once more disappear back to wherever he'd been, and ignore the children again, often for several days.

The creeping around the house was a new thing, however. Again, over time, the children got used to his sudden appearances, but much less so to the fright of coming upon him in odd locations, looking shifty. There was no other word to describe it, either; we'd catch him wandering around the outside of the house in the dark, and peering into the windows, watching how we were all behaving. This was extremely unsettling, particularly for the younger children, who never knew where he might pop up next.

Paul was also becoming obsessed with finding out what we might be saying about him. By now, we'd not shared a bedroom for several years, and Jamie, now in her early teens, would often come into mine and snuggle up for a chat. We'd have the usual kinds of girlie conversations. Talking about boys, about school work, about anything and everything, as mums do with teenage daughters everywhere.

On this particular night, at around 11pm, we were sitting on my bed chatting, when Jamie thought she heard something overhead.

'Can you hear something, mum?' she asked me, mid-sentence. 'It sounds like there's someone on the roof.'

I listened too. And she was right. My bedroom by this time was in the part of the house that had been extended and had a flat roof, and there were sounds as if someone was walking around over our heads. They then stopped, just above us, so after waiting a few moments, I crept silently to the window, stuck out my head and looked up, and, sure enough, there was Paul, his face illuminated white in the moonlight, lying on his stomach with his head hanging down above the lintel.

'What on earth are you doing?' I asked, as he scrabbled back out of view. 'Wasp's nest,' came the muffled reply as he disappeared. Which I might have swallowed had not a similar thing have happened a couple of nights later when, again, we heard a noise, this time down on the gravel, and when I peered out of the window I found him stationed against the house wall, clearly trying to eavesdrop on our conversation.

It's ironic, looking back, to try and analyse these behaviours, and to understand that he was paranoid that we might be talking about him. Ironic because he wasn't ever a topic of conversation during these sessions, though it was certainly true that as I emotionally detached myself from him, he was beginning to direct his rages more and more towards his eldest daughter – a major factor in the decision I would soon take.

There was no question that Paul was paranoid generally. The rather childish sense that everyone who wronged him was 'out to get him' that I'd observed when I'd first met him, had, over the years, morphed into something stronger and more focused. It was no longer just a case of people having it in for him. He believed his phone was being tapped and that he was regularly being followed. He also lied to trick us into doing the things he wanted - something that would only become fully apparent after his death, when his many diaries revealed a very different truth.

He would lie for what seemed like no reason, as well. One day, in 2005, very close to Christmas, I'd planned a trip to take the children to see their Nanna Brenda, my now elderly father's second wife, and who we only saw once a year. I should perhaps have expected trouble even before we went, because Paul hadn't wanted us to go. With the exception of his parents, he was increasingly trying to stop contact with all our relatives, including both our brothers, for reasons that would only become fully clear after his death. Right now though, it now only served to heighten our isolation, as we had so little in the way of family in the first place.

I was determined I was going on this visit, however, as with my brood growing, I was becoming increasingly aware of how few living relatives they had to call their own. But I wasn't in the least surprised when, halfway into the journey to Brackley, about an hour's drive away, my mobile rang.

'I'm locked out,' he said flatly, after I'd managed to pull up at the side of the busy road, switched off the engine and returned the call. 'Where are you?'

'You know where I am,' I pointed out, because he did. He knew full well we'd planned a Christmas visit to Nanny Brenda's that evening.

'Well, you need to turn around and come back again,' he said. 'Or I'll be stuck out here in the cold all night.'

It was ridiculous; we were almost halfway there by then. And I also knew full well that he wasn't locked out. He'd been locked out many times over the years, and would tell me with pride all his ways of getting back into the house – which windows he used; his various clever ways of doing it. So the one thing I knew he would not being doing at any point that evening was sitting shivering on the doorstep. Not till it served his purposes, that was. But to call him a liar was tantamount to lunacy, so I went along with it. 'Go to a coffee shop then,' I suggested. 'Get something to eat and drink. Read a book.'

He wasn't having that. He hadn't wanted us to go and he wanted us to come back. And what he wanted took precedence over everything. 'I'll just have to sit in the van and wait for you then,' he huffed, presumably expecting me to cave in and turn around.

But, physically separated from him, and with a car load of children, I wasn't going to be manipulated on this occasion. 'Fine,' I said, conceding as little ground as I could. 'We'll try not to leave it late coming back.'

The visit made and curtailed with the thought of him fuming at home completely spoiling it, we headed back much earlier than planned. And, sure enough, when we arrived back he was sitting there in the company van, visibly shivering, and making such a big thing of it that the older children were even cross that I'd not turned around as he had asked.

But when I let him in and went into the kitchen, I went straight to the kettle, and, as I'd suspected, it was hot to the touch. Not that I would be tempted to challenge him in a million years, however many 'points' I could score by exposing him. It wouldn't help the children and it certainly wouldn't help me, because he could turn violent in the blink of an eye, even without a shred of provocation, so to actually provide some would be foolhardy in the extreme.

Paul was also becoming increasingly devious about money. My brother Tony, who still lived in care, was too autistic to hold down a job, but was never short of money as he very rarely spent any. When one of Tony's insurance policies matured and Paul found out about it, he wasted no time in deciding he needed to borrow it – all £20,000. I was totally against this, not least because it was my brother and I had no idea how we'd ever pay it back, but that was never going to stop Paul doing anything. Sure enough, he drew up a 'contract' – a document securing the money Tony lent him against a piece of woodland we owned near the house. It was only a matter of months, however, before Paul decided to sell the piece of woodland, meaning the deal wasn't worth the paper it was written on.

It would turn out to be the tip of a huge, undiscovered iceberg.

I was in the biscuit aisle in the local pound shop in 2004 when it came to me that I had to put an end to this travesty of a family life. I was in a world of my own, having just seen a sticker on the back of a parked car that said 'One Life. Live It!' It was one of those light bulb moments that stay with you forever. I had one life and I definitely wasn't living it – not the way I should have been, anyway.

It was a kind of epiphany; a falling into place of so many pieces of a jigsaw, that had been forced into holes where they absolutely didn't fit. There was nothing wrong with my mind; I had simply been brainwashed, and the only person who was allowing that to continue to happen was me. What did it matter that the outside world thought Paul was perfect? They didn't *know* him. And why should I care what the world thought of me? I knew the truth, and the truth made for uncomfortable viewing. I was living a life that wasn't a life at all.

And it wasn't as if I was trapped in it – I wasn't. I might think I was – I had convinced myself of that for two decades, in fact - but I wasn't. Not physically, anyway. And in thinking that, I wondered why I'd never realised that before. It would be complicated, yes, but could it really be worse than staying? One thing was certain – though Paul's damaging effect on the children was still unknowable, if I stayed with him much longer, worse would surely follow; I would soon be rendered worse than useless as their mother.

I don't know what prompted that moment of clarity. But I suddenly knew I had the will to leave Paul and see it through. Our marriage was dead. We were done. It was over.

PART TWO

CHAPTER TWENTY-ONE
DADDY'S GONE

15th September 2007

Paul was dead. We were done. It was over.

'I'm sorry,' the doctor told me. 'There was nothing I could do.'

I stared at him, not seeing, not quite believing it. But it was true. He was gone. But like this?

I had no words in my head to describe the myriad emotions that bombarded my brain when I the doctor said those words to me. My mind began racing then; I knew the children had to be told, but in the most gentle way possible – not just blurted out when I was still in shock myself.

'What will happen now?' I asked the doctor, through a blur of tears and panic.

'The coroner's van will come now and take away the body,' he told me quietly.

'The children can't see that.' I couldn't allow that to happen. Even in my confused state, that conviction was a strong one. 'I must take them away before it comes.'

'I agree,' the doctor said. 'Is there anywhere you could all go? Someone you know, who'll be able to support you all?'

Vicki, I thought, her name springing to mind immediately. I knew she and her husband Craig had only arrived back from holiday first thing that morning, but I also knew she would be there for us, because she was my dearest and closest friend. I gave her number to one of the policemen and he told me to leave him to it – he would call her, explain what had happened, and ask if they could take us all over there to her. She and Craig must have been shattered, but, thankfully, she agreed.

While that was being organised, the officer in charge told me, as gently as he could, that there was a lot of blood around the car, and they would do their best to wash it away so the children didn't see it. It was yet another example of the care and compassion everyone had shown us, and I was so grateful but, of course, there was nothing they could do to change the facts of Paul's messy, violent suicide.

The children were, naturally, bewildered. I lied to them and told them that Daddy was 'alive but only just' and that he had now been taken to hospital. I knew all I was doing was buying a few hours in which to gather my thoughts and strength, and to soften the blow – whenever it came – by having them consider the prospect that he might die in hospital. Was that the right decision? I'll never know. I was trying to cope minute by minute, and it felt right at the time, even if it meant that over the ensuing hours the stress of knowing the job still had to be done was terrible.

That done, we then gathered ourselves to be taken over to Vicki's; some of the children in the van and the rest – if reluctantly, on the part of the police – travelling with me in the Previa.

Fighting to hold on in the blur of raw emotion I was feeling, I was also acutely aware that I needed to call back the client who'd telephoned about his missing equipment that morning. It felt so long ago now but he was presumably still waiting patiently – or perhaps, impatiently – for a call. It also popped into my brain that we had another event that night to sort out. We were supposed to be providing a roulette table for a lady's 30th birthday party and, even in the sea of terror in which I was swimming, it occurred to me that I must not let her down.

I have no idea why I fixated so intently on that one thing when we reached Vicki's; so strange the way our brains work sometimes. Perhaps I was just clinging on to some vestige of normality by focusing on my business responsibilities. Who knows? But what I do know is that once I'd phoned the first man, I became obsessed with getting the second event sorted, trying to think of a solution to the problem, racking my brains to think who I could ring.

Particularly galling was that it had been one that Paul had planned to do on his own, so there wasn't even a contingency arranged. In a desperate effort to sort something out, I called a guy called Geoff, who ran a company called Leisure Hire. They were the suppliers of the high tech equipment we didn't own ourselves, and at the same time one of the clients who hired the giant games from us, and over the years we'd built up quite a friendship.

I managed to reach him on his mobile and blurted everything out, and, like everyone else, he was shocked at what he was hearing. He also did his best: he couldn't do it himself, but tried hard to find someone else who could do it for us. He had no success, however, so the next thing I did was call the lady herself and apologise for letting her down. Again, she was shocked – I just said Paul had died, rather than mention suicide – but she was incredibly kind and understanding.

As soon as I put the phone down, it started ringing. And it carried on ringing almost non-stop. Geoff again, the police, various mums of friends of the kids. The wave of support was overwhelming and non-stop, but I couldn't take anything in.

We'd arrived at Vicki's house at about 12.30, and as the minutes inched slowly by, my principal memory was of knowing she was so shattered – she'd not slept all night and must have been dropping on her feet – but that she managed to stay so calm and focused; was the rock to which we all so desperately needed to cling. She made beans on toast – it seemed like tins and tins of beans were gobbled up – and in the midst of this, at 2pm, the Police called to let me know that though Paul's body had been moved from where he had been found in the pond down in the woods, the whole area, plus the car and area around that too were a potential crime scene and that we mustn't go near them. 'Not that I would anyway,' the officer warned. 'Particularly the car, because there's quite a lot of blood in and around it, of course.'

I seized on that call. Grim thought it was, it was also an opportunity to buy myself a little further time and help prepare the children for the horror that still lay ahead. I pretended that the hospital had called with the news that Paul was alive but in an extremely critical state, and that they didn't think he was going to survive. They were desperately upset, obviously, but still clung on to hope, but though it was so painful to see that hope etched on their faces, knowing the truth, I still felt strongly that telling them in stages would help them be just a little more prepared for the truth when it came.

Was I right? Once again, to this day, I don't know. But at the time it felt very much like the kindest thing to do. Not that I was making things easy for myself, because as the afternoon wore on – such a hot, sunny, perfect sort of day – I could only look on in agony while the children, who'd now spilled out into Vicki's garden, ran around and played, or became engrossed in TV, to take their minds off the worry and the waiting.

It was a call from Paul's brother Peter that nudged me into facing the inevitable. I knew Paul's parents knew Paul had tried to kill himself, at least, because it was a call Jamie had made before we'd left for Vicki's. And the news had obviously been passed on to Peter. He'd been having surgery on his shoulder that morning, and I'd learn later on that his girlfriend, Lorraine, had told him the minute he'd come round after the operation. He was now, understandably, completely distraught, and as I told him the same thing as Jamie had told their father – that we were waiting for news still, I felt terrible about not telling him the truth.

But there was no way I could do that before telling the children, so, however hard it was going to be tell them I must.

'I've got to do it now,' I told Vicki, after speaking to Peter.

'Do you want a drink first, to steel your nerves?' she asked.

I shook my head. It didn't feel right to tell the children with alcohol inside me, somehow, but I did need a crutch. On an instinct that shocked me, I reached instead for Craig's packet of cigarettes. I hadn't smoked in 18 years, and I knew I shouldn't now, but the need to do so now was suddenly overwhelming, even though as soon as I'd finished smoking it I wished I hadn't. Now I simply felt nauseous as well as distressed.

My phone rang once more. It was the police again, to let me know that there would have to be a post mortem, and asking if I would be able to identify Paul's body at the mortuary on the Monday. It was another grim thought, but, again, the timing was perfect. I could pretend it was the hospital, to tell me Paul had passed away.

I came off the phone and, with Vicki at my side, assembled the children into a group in the garden. I'll never forget their little faces all looking up at me so expectantly, praying that I was going to tell them that daddy was going to be fine and that life would return to as near normal as it had ever been for them. My heart was breaking for them and at the same time I was terrified of what the future would hold; I felt the weight of so much responsibility - sitting right there in front of me - and I was about to break the worst imaginable news.

I tried to be as gentle as I could. 'That was the hospital… I'm so sorry, but daddy has passed away… they did their best but there was nothing they could do to save him…' But how can you break news of that kind gently?

There are no words. And, as I'd suspected, their reaction was both instant and horrific. Every one of them screamed. Disbelief mingled with horror. Faces full of terror looked back at me, contorted, testament to the breaking of their tiny hearts. All I could do was try to hold as many of them at once as was physically possible, and I was so grateful that I'd asked Vicki to sit by my side; that they felt close enough to her to allow her to help me comfort them.

Kacie ran off, then. She was 13 and had already seen things she shouldn't have had to and I was torn, then – did I go after her and stay with the others? Allow her some space? Thirteen is such a difficult age. But my instinct said no, that I needed to go and find her, so while Vicki stayed with the others I ran off in pursuit, and eventually, once Craig and their son Loz had joined in the search, we found her in some woods next to their house.

She just kept screaming the word 'NO', over and over. She couldn't take any of it in and I could see how bewildered she was. She'd been with Jamie when they went down to the car and found the note, and had already experienced so much trauma, and I knew this could push her over the edge. But the others needed me too, and, blessedly, between us, we managed to regain some composure.

By this time I'd managed to forget my own feelings and was just in a blind panic trying to get the children through. But how do you help anyone through something so terrible? Where do you begin? They were all so young. It was impossible and I think a part of me accepted that even then. Only time would heal such deep gaping wounds.

We stayed with Vicki for another couple of hours and then I decided we should all head home. None of us wanted to go back there, but I also knew we had no choice. It was too much to expect Vicki to put up all eight of us, and a part of me felt that, however grim the prospect, our home was the place the children needed to sleep. A place none of us wanted to be but there was no choice.

It was a silent drive back. No one had anything to say, because there *was* nothing to say. Not yet. However, once we arrived home, and my friend Ingrid turned up to see if she could help, there was suddenly lots of talk, which was an incredible blessing, as was her help getting the younger children to bed. She also returned the next day with a plan to take us out – something that might seem an odd thing to be doing, but was, in fact, the thing we probably needed most, because it was a Sunday and there was nothing practical I could do.

Ingrid arrived the following morning, as promised, and took us all to Kenilworth Castle. The whole thing was a blur but perhaps it was a necessary blur – we were shell-shocked and still unable to properly process what had happened, and it was certainly better than sitting around the house, and I was incredibly grateful for her support, as I was for that of two other friends, Fiona and Simon, parents of one of Lorie and Mirie's friends, who came round when we returned and cooked a meal for us.

For someone who'd grown up in such a troubled, isolated family, I felt overwhelmed by the kindness that was shown to us that weekend; it was like the planting of a seed that would grow into a seedling of strength that would begin to see me – see all of us – through the nightmare.

Monday morning dawned and there was no question of the children going to school, so I began what would become a sort of Groundhog Day of pain, as each school needed to be phoned and the situation explained, the same expressions of shock and sympathy listened to. And with each step on that road, our new reality was hammered home; Paul had gone, and so had every certainty, positive or negative. What on earth were we going to do now?

I was profoundly grateful to see Vicki and Fiona arrive at 10am, along with a lady called Beth from a company called Take a Break, who provided short respite care for the three younger children. Beth also came bearing a bag of food and supplies, for which, once again, I was extremely grateful because I had almost no money at all. The question now, of course, was where was I going to find some? It was a question I could now begin trying to address, which I needed to do as a matter of urgency.

Paul had put the house on the market back in June. We were in so much debt there was nothing else we could do. We had managed to get a reasonable price for it, too, but we were now locked in a round of solicitors' letters because Paul wanted to pay everyone straight off at the time of the sale, and my solicitor was adamant that couldn't and wouldn't happen as it would leave me and the children without any money to live on at all.

By this time we had arranged to move into rented accommodation – the children and I into one place and Paul into another; a point on which I was adamant I would not budge. By now the children were so badly affected by his mood swings, unpredictability, coldness and aggression, that I could no longer countenance him living close to them.

At this point we'd not yet exchanged contracts on the sale, but one thing I knew was that the people who were buying the house wanted us out within the next four weeks. This meant a decision needed to be made, and needed to be made fast – something I felt wholly unable to do. My brain couldn't even decide whether I should have a cup of coffee, so deciding whether to try to go ahead with the sale was impossible.

I rang the estate agent to put them in the picture, but, in reality, there was little they could suggest.

'Well, you can pull out,' came the response. 'There's nothing to stop you doing that, obviously. But without money to pay the mortgage, I don't see how you will be able to stay there, either.' All of which confirmed what I already knew. As did the call to the mortgage company, the second mortgage company and what was beginning to feel like the whole world. The bottom had certainly dropped out of ours.

I literally didn't have a penny to my name so I'd phoned our Social Worker, to get her advice as far possible, because I knew she'd be able to help us. She'd been involved with us for 18 months, brought in at the request of the CAMHS, the Child and Adolescent Mental Health Service. That she was part of our lives had been one of the big sources of conflict during that time, as, despite it being standard practice for families with so many children with special needs, Paul hated the stigma of 'having' a social worker. For me, however, her support had been invaluable, allowing me to find ways to get my life on some sort of track for the future, as well as saving me from drowning emotionally. She'd also been the one to bring Beth from Take a Break into our lives, allowing me four hours a week that were incredibly precious; meaning I could go to Tesco without having them in tow.

I got through and got straight to the point. What would happen if I didn't go ahead with the sale of the house but eventually had to give the keys back to the Building Society? The answer that came back was chilling. I would have made myself and the children voluntarily homeless and in that situation the council wouldn't re-house us. I couldn't believe what I was hearing. I felt totally trapped and hopeless. What should I do? What was the best way out of this mess? I hadn't an idea in my head, and didn't know how to find one, because none of the information that was coming my way was helping me to decide.

One thing that was clear was that I still needed to formally identify Paul's body, something that wasn't apparently going to happen that day after all. The assistant coroner wanted to be there, apparently, and as she couldn't make it, it was scheduled for 11am on the Tuesday.

I was dreading it, so when Vicki offered to come along with me I was once again eternally grateful to her for her unerring support. Indeed, for *all* my friends' support. Between them Vicki, Ingrid and Fiona had made sure the children ate, had tidied the house as best they could and were pulling together to keep things as 'normal' as possible.

I felt for them because I knew how helpless they all really felt and I couldn't make them feel any better apart from thanking them at every opportunity. Looking back, that in itself must have driven them mad.

On the Tuesday morning all three turned up again, Fiona busying herself making endless lists of things I needed to do, Ingrid trying to keep the kids going and Vicki - ever the practical one - walking around, broom in hand, cleaning. When the time came to leave for the mortuary we then got into Vicki's car and drove the 15 minutes to Warwick Hospital.

It took a while to find the mortuary – it was a place no-one would want to know the location of, after all – and when we rang the bell it was as if we'd stepped straight into another world, because Lurch opened the door to us. Literally. If ever a person looked like they fitted their job description, then this mortuary assistant did. It was a shock and, perhaps because I was already on the edge, I immediately had the feeling I was walking into a horror movie, and was terrified of what I was about to see.

And then we waited. The assistant coroner had arranged to meet us there so we sat in the waiting room and duly did so. Time passed. It was 11.15am and then 11.30am, and when there was no sign of her by 11.35am, Lurch came in, reigniting the jitters I was trying so hard to quash, and offered to ring her to see where she was.

He came back with the news that he hadn't been able to get hold of her and that we would have to wait a little longer. It was becoming intolerable for me, despite Vicki's attempts to calm me, because the longer we waited the sharper were the images invading in my brain, and the more my mind became overwhelmed with the reality of my life now – that a few feet away from me was my husband who was dead and I was going to have to look at him and I wasn't sure I felt able to. My anxiety levels, already sky-high from the events of the previous three days, were now going strato-spheric. I needed this to be over with – the waiting was making me feel as though I couldn't get through another minute of my life.

It was 11.40am when Lurch returned again, though it had felt like so much longer, to tell us we could go ahead and identify Paul's body without the coroner after all, and take us through to the mortuary itself. The sense of being in a horror film only increased.

It looked like it had been decorated, unsuccessfully, to feel like a 'friendly' environment, but in fact, it just felt dark, forbidding and morbid. Looking back, perhaps there is no way to achieve what they'd set out to in such a place and situation, but, even more unfortunate was the immedi-ate dank, musty smell. It hit me as soon as Lurch opened the door and into the (equally misjudged, to my mind) dark burgundy colour scheme.

There was a hospital trolley parked to the right of the gloomy room, with the shape of a body – presumably Paul's – under a sheet. Lurch walked around to the other side of it, while I hung back, transfixed and terrified, by the door. Then, without warning, he simply pulled it back from Paul's head and shoulders.

The expression 'weak at the knees' is a cliché for good reason. I really did feel my legs were going to buckle under me. I'd seen dead bodies before – both my mother, when I was sixteen, and, more recently, my father's, but I had never seen anything like this.

Waves of shock and nausea overcame me as I looked at him. His face was contorted into the most grotesque mask of agony I could possibly imagine. His mouth was gaping open to the point where I could see every tooth and filling and his eyes, equally wide, had an expression locked into them of someone who has just witnessed the most evil horror imaginable. I thought I was going to be sick but held on as best I could, as the tears poured unchecked down my cheeks.

I wanted to hang back but something seemed to be pulling me; drawing me closer to his body like some kind of invisible force. Despite the horror of what I was seeing, I felt compelled to get nearer, even if my conscious mind could think only one thing – that despite the fact that, to live, I had to free myself from this man, his decision to die was like a body blow. I was now alone in the world and felt completely helpless. I was only inches away from his face when Lurch asked, in a still voice, 'Is this the body of Paul Shanks?'

'Yes' I managed to get out, hardly audibly. He put the sheet back over Paul's face then and gestured for us to go but something kept me rooted to the spot. I knew then, and can confirm now, that the trauma of seeing Paul like that would be an image that would stay in my head forever. It was just so shocking. I had expected seeing his body to be hard but, at the same time, I had an expectation of what I'd be seeing – a body, yes, but one composed as my parents had been – waxy, yes, but at least at peace.

There was no peace to be found here. Vicki, too, was looking horrified, tears rolling down her cheeks, and I felt a surge of guilt for having accepted her offer and put her through such a horrendous experience with no warning as well. How could it be that no one had warned us that he would be as he was the moment he drew his last breath? Why hadn't someone who knew about such things told us to be prepared? Maybe if the assistant coroner had turned up it would have been different; perhaps she would have taken us aside and done just that, but she didn't and it wasn't and we were deeply traumatised.

We walked quickly back to the car, Vicki trying desperately to be strong for me, suggesting as we got back to it that we go for a coffee somewhere, so we could at least try to compose ourselves. But it was too much. I had no words. And, without my consciously anticipating it, I began screaming and I couldn't seem to stop. I was hysterical, pure and simple – me, who'd been so strong all these years. I had no idea how to carry on myself, never mind trying to carry the children through it all as well.

CHAPTER TWENTY-TWO
A LIFE LAID BARE

Returning from identifying Paul's body marked a mental transition. I was on my own now, and it really was beginning to sink in. Though we returned to find that Ingrid and Fiona had been beavering away, trying to get to grips with everything, the reality – which took the form of an ever growing list of things that only I could deal with – was making me feel more frightened by the minute. They were right to do so, because I couldn't hide away and pretend it wasn't happening, but with every new item added, I felt worse and worse. I had seven small people relying on me totally, but how could I possibly go on?

I had no idea just how bad things were, but I could only think in the moment, and one of the main priorities was to sort out the appalling state of our finances in the short term, just so that we could function day to day. So, to that end, I rang a government financial hotline designed to be there for people who urgently needed money, but was told that because my child benefit was due in ten days I didn't qualify for a short-term loan.

I put the phone down feeling desperate. I had about £15 in my purse and absolutely nothing else, and was already having to accept charity; Vicki, Ingrid and Fiona were buying us the essentials out of their own pockets. I couldn't bear to let that continue, but didn't know where else to turn, so I was grateful beyond words when Ingrid's husband Lee came to the rescue, by offering to lend me some money until at least my child benefit came through. He turned out to be my life saver in the months that followed, and in so many different ways, and I have no idea how I would be here now if it weren't for him. For any of them. I was very, very blessed.

It would be wrong to say the pain eased as the days went by because it didn't. Pain and trauma of that magnitude don't just fade away, but we did settle into a kind of way of living minute by minute and I was amazed at the strength of some of the children when, as that first shocking week drew to a close, they announced they wanted to return to school. Lorie was first - reasoning that as she had to get it over with at some point it might as well be sooner rather than later. I agreed with her; the longer they left it the harder it would surely get.

My own days, meanwhile, were spent contacting various official bodies, both to notify them of Paul's death and to change everything into my name, the paperwork for which was horrendous. Doing all of this meant regular visits to the Atlas, down in the field, where Paul had not only set up his home for the past three years, but also his office. I hated having to go in and seeing all of his things just as he had left them, but everything I needed seemed to be in there.

I was grateful, therefore, when Paul's brother Peter came up to visit about ten days after Paul's death, as soon as he was well enough following his shoulder operation. Peter and I had become closer over the years and our relationship was very good - a state of affairs that closely correlated with the worsening relationship he had with his older brother. I felt enormously sorry for him, feeling Paul's reasons for being so unkind to him had always been weak, bordering on spurious. Peter was a great uncle to his nieces and nephew and one of the first things he told me following Paul's suicide was that I could rely on him - as far as he was able, of course - to step into Paul's shoes for them. He was a rock for all of us, and in those first foggy days and weeks, as well as discussing all the practical things, we had many emotional conversations about Paul and our need to find answers to so many questions, chief among them why he had taken his own life.

We were about to find out. Though the weather was beginning to turn autumnal, the sun was still warm on our backs when we walked down to the Atlas that September afternoon, a few of the older children coming along as well. The caravan was parked on concrete hard-standing in the corner of one of the fields, on which had previously stood a wooden field shelter for the horses. The roof of that had long since gone and just the structure remained, with the concrete floor gradually being overrun by weeds. It was that time of year when, summer's growth having not quite given way to autumn, the grass and plants were at their most overgrown, and there was a sharp but not unpleasant smell of damp foliage in the air, along with the distinctive musty aroma from the fungus that was growing on the wood.

The caravan wasn't locked – there was no longer any point in my doing so - so Peter turned the handle on the side door to let us in, allowing the warm heavy interior air to escape. By this time Paul was using the sitting room of the Atlas as his home, and he had kept his living quarters very Spartan. The area where he slept was very sparse with only a table lamp beside the bed, and a few personal bits neatly arranged. The kitchen, too, held very little. A few plates and cups and bowls, a single loaf of decaying bread – all laid out with absolute precision.

He'd had turned what would have been the master bedroom into his office, having removed the bed and built a basic desk and shelves. Everything in there was meticulously organised, too, and I wondered what Peter must be thinking now he was seeing things that had obviously become normal for us as a family but might make him see his older brother in a different light. Pens and pencils lined up in rows, with geometric precision; the accounts books, all identical, perfectly piled up in date order; ring binders, rows of them, exactly the same, with the name on each written at precisely the same level, having been painstakingly measured with a ruler; neat piles of spiral bound reporter's notebooks, with the covers ripped off; something Paul had always done before using them. The same attention to detail applied to his diaries; a whole decade's worth of which stood like soldiers lined up for inspection, ordered by date, with the sticker on each at exactly the same height on the spine.

With Paul's diaries having been such a longstanding part of him I had, over the years, normalised them too. And, initially, objectively, there was nothing strange about them; they were the tools with which he kept track of his work and business dealings, a source of order that seemed not at all dysfunctional. In that sense, we had always been chalk and cheese, Paul and I. Though less exacting in matters physical, I have a well-ordered brain, and keep track of things largely in my head. Paul, on the other hand, for all his obsession with minimalism, and for all the severity of his OCD, found keeping balls in the air mentally much harder, and his thinking could often be chaotic. It had therefore one of his 'things' from early on, to buy a new diary every year and to spend hours ruling it up on New Year's Day. He'd do everything with a ruler, and was precise in every measurement; columns, rows, and various other forms of sub-division would be demarcated, ready to record the events and transactions of the coming years. And whatever helped him to cope was fine with me.

As the years had passed, however, so had the contents of the diaries. They had evolved into what ended up to be a very different species of tool from the one I had first seen him filling in, back in the eighties. And as I gazed at them again now, I realised that, should I delve into them in order, I might be able to chart the inexorable decline in his sanity. I certainly recalled when I'd first found them worrying; when the neatly recorded details of meetings and transactions had begun being swamped by an almost incomprehensible system of multi-coloured highlighting, of equally incomprehensible hastily scribbled notes, the contents of which were often so bizarre.

It had been rare for me by that time to question anything Paul did, but, prompted by concerns that this was no longer remotely 'normal', I once asked him why he felt the need to record every single moment of his day.

'It's a time and motion study,' came the prompt, predictably irritable response. 'I'm just trying to work out where my time is going, obviously.'

I hadn't asked him again.

Before Paul's death, I hadn't set foot in the Atlas in three or four years, and every time I entered now I felt this intense claustrophobia, seeing the evidence of Paul's latter life laid bare. It was also stuffy and cramped in the office part – it was a typical caravan bedroom - so Peter and I decided to take piles of paperwork, bit by bit, and go through them while sitting on the bed in the living room. It was while we were doing so that Kacie handed a reporter's notebook to me.

'Mum, you need to look at this,' she said quietly.

I'd already been through several of the piles of notebooks that had been dotted around the office space, and made a mental note to come back to them later. Paul had always had several of them on the go at one time, although I was very rarely privy to their contents. On closer inspection every one contained pretty much the same thing; endless lists of potential solutions to our financial problems, clients who needed contacting, potential schemes for borrowing more money and so on. We'd also already found four large boxes full of junk mail related to potential loans from hundreds of different companies.

The look on Kacie's face told me this reporter's pad might be different, so I opened it and started skimming the contents of the first page. And as I did so, I felt a chill that was at odds with the clement weather, and hoped she hadn't herself read too much.

In time I would find out that she had not only read it – as had Jamie – but that she'd first hidden it, too, anxious to protect me. But she'd changed her mind, deciding that perhaps it was something I *should* see.

Paul had spent his life making plans; it was an unremitting constant. As was the fact that few ever came to fruition. And as I read, what impressed itself upon me most strongly was my profound gratitude that this plan had gone the way of most of the others, because here, in black and white, recorded in his singular, miniscule handwriting, was evidence of the true horror of Paul's sick and twisted mind. Page after page was filled with incredibly detailed plans about how he intended to kill me and all the children, and then himself.

I could hardly believe what was right before my eyes. He had it mapped it out minutely, right down to the precise times and details; how he was going to threaten all the children that he was going to hurt me, in order to keep them under control. He'd also planned to then lock them all in their bedrooms, causing me to remember something with a sickened jolt. Suddenly, the bolts he'd put high up on the *outside* of every bedroom door two years previously, made sense. We'd all wondered why he'd done it at the time – the older girls especially – and never thought to question his apparently logical answer that it would mean we'd be able to lock the cats out.

I knew I would need to remove then as a matter of urgency. Just the thought of them being there was too upsetting. And as I read on, it was to find that Paul's planning was equally thorough in almost every respect. He'd mused about how best to kill us all, in what order and where, his plan of choice seeming to be to kill every child, one by one, in front of me, so that I witnessed their deaths before being killed myself. He would then, according to his notes, kill himself.

A few days before Paul's death, I had come down one morning to find that both my laptop and the company computer were missing. It had been infuriating, as I had an audition for the then TV programme, *Ten Years Younger*, and needed the details on the email in order to advance-book a train. Paul was nowhere to be found either, so I'd called him on his mobile only to find he'd taken them to his parents to have 'someone hack into them to find out what you're doing behind my back.'

As I stood there now, surrounded by evidence of what he'd been doing behind *our* backs, the chilling irony of his words didn't escape me.

Various doctors over the last few years have suggested that Paul might have been suffering from a Dissociative Identity Disorder (DID), which might explain why he kept his minute-by-minute diaries. Were the thoughts spelled out in them those of one of his identities? Was the 'other Paul' the one who had decided to end his life? I'll never know the answer, and perhaps I wouldn't even had he lived, but the children take comfort from believing that his good self ended his life to save us from his evil side.

Despite the horror inherent in finding out what might have been via that reporter's notebook, my discovery in the Atlas was cathartic. Because it dawned on me that the fear we had all experienced, and for so many years, had actually been very well-founded. And, towards the end, that fear had become really intense. My bedroom was above the back door and if it opened in the night it would wake me up immediately. Once we'd agreed to split, and Paul had made his temporary home up in the Atlas, hearing that sound would never fail to make my heart thump. I would lay there in the dark, then, catching my breath, praying silently that he wouldn't come upstairs and start attacking me verbally or physically.

All those years of being at odds with the wider world's view of my husband. All those times when I questioned myself, despite the mounting evidence. All those situations when I re-wrote the script, according to Paul. All history.

Peter was as shocked by the notebook as we were. He also agreed to my request that he take it home and store it somewhere, so that there was no danger of the other children ever finding it. It was the last thing I ever wanted any of them to see; I was troubled enough that Jamie and Kacie had already.

I knew what I'd read would be indelibly printed on my own brain, however, and had to try and push it to the back of my mind. There was still much to do, and I was equally grateful for Peter's support in coming to the undertakers with me. He stayed with us for two days, and by the time he returned home, all the big decisions about the funeral had been made. We had plenty of time, because the Post Mortem took a lot longer than we had expected and it would be a day short of three weeks before the funeral took place. Under the circumstances, it felt like an eternity.

There was more distressing trauma yet to come, though. As soon as I was notified that his body had finally been released to the funeral home Jamie, then 16 years old, had started asking to go and see her father. I was very much against it. I'd been exactly the same age when my mother had died, and I had always regretted my decision to go and see her at the chapel of rest. My most enduring image, still, is of her lying dead in her coffin, rather than other, happier memories of her in life.

I felt it essential that I get this through to Jamie, but her autism kicked in and she took a position of opposition, and was more determined to see Paul than ever – something, despite my experience and relative maturity, that I knew I had no right to deny her. I went to speak to Noel at the funeral home, to ask her advice. As I'd suspected, she said she would strongly recommend that none of the children saw him.

I accepted Noel's wisdom, as it chimed with my own, but Jamie was relentless. And the more she pushed, the more the other children came around to her way of thinking; they wanted to see Paul one last time too. Within days, the whole thing was spiralling out of control with tears of grief being shed along with tears of uncontrollable hysteria; all part of the shock of the tragedy, of course, but when even Peter's intervention failed to make Jamie see reason, I caved in and went back to Noel to see if it could be organised, despite every bone in my body yelling no. After all, would my refusal to let the children say goodbye create more damaging scars than there would be already?

Possibly, but Noel was still adamant. As I sat opposite her, she leaned forward and couldn't have made her feelings plainer. It was a *very* bad idea for Jamie to see him. 'But she's so desperate to,' I said, explaining just how hard I'd tried to dissuade her, and of reaching the conclusion that to deny her what she so seemed to need might be even more distressing for her. 'For better or worse,' I said, 'Jamie, at least, *has* to be allowed to.'

But Noel's face told me that there was another reason she was not going to give in. 'What *is* it?' I asked. 'Is there something you're not telling me?'

She then told me, in the gentlest tones, that there was indeed something else. With the time delay, Paul's body had deteriorated badly, and though they had sorted his facial features out, and would cover up the cuts on his neck and the vivid bruising on his face with make-up, what couldn't be concealed was the smell. Even the process of embalming couldn't take the smell away, she told me, at the same time assuring me that it was horrific. That clinched it.

Jamie didn't mention it when she returned from school that evening, and hope briefly rose in me that she'd perhaps changed her mind. But no, when she came into my bedroom for a cuddle and chat that evening, 'did you go to the undertakers?' was the first thing she asked.

Her response to my confirmation that I had, and that they'd still told me no, was another bout of uncontrollable hysterics. He was *her* dad, she railed at me, and she had every right to see him - and she needed to see him in order to accept in her own mind that he really was dead.

The worst part of it was that I totally agreed. It was her right and it wasn't up to me to stop her. Yet, come what may, I simply couldn't let it happen. So round and round we went, for best part of an hour, when it finally became clear to me that nothing I said would work, and all I could do was tell her the gruesome truth. I tried to be gentle – using words like 'deteriorate' and 'hard to look at', all of which she batted right back at me. She was strong enough, she was prepared, she could deal with it, it didn't matter. She still wanted to see him for herself.

In the end, all out of ideas, I told her the truth; that his body had started to break down - to rot - and the funeral director could do nothing about the horrific smell. The news shocked her into silence and she stared at me. Then after a few seconds, she began to sob again, falling into my arms and staying there for several long hours, crying enough tears to last a lifetime.

I felt her pain so desperately.

CHAPTER TWENTY-THREE
PANDORA'S BOX

Finding the notes Paul had written on the reporter's pad turned out to be just the start of a process that would take years to recover from. But in the short term, I had to deal with practicalities. Trying to sort the financial mess we had been left with was my number one priority, so while we existed in that post-mortem limbo before the funeral, I set about doing just that.

First of all, I had to look at our regular outgoings. And chief among them was one that had been going out for many years now, just to maintain three separate 40ft storage units, some 10 miles away. These were an obsession with Paul, I knew, though had no idea of the extent of it. But whatever it was, my friend Lee, Ingrid's husband, said we must clear them immediately because they were costing £500 a month.

I had an unimaginable mess to sort out. Once we'd located the keys for the padlocks, it was Lee who drove me over there, about ten days after Paul's death. All three containers Paul had been renting were full size 40ft ones; massive shipping containers, of the kind you see massed on quaysides, bound for cargo ships. The scale of them, close up, was mind-blowing.

We took a breath and dived straight in. And the first container we opened wasn't too much of a shock as it contained most of the games equipment and a lot of boxes at the back, so was no great surprise to see.

The second, however, was different. This one was chock-full of cardboard boxes, stacked neatly from floor to ceiling, running the entire length of the unit, with a gap in the middle that was just wide enough to walk down. I couldn't imagine what on earth was inside them.

I was soon to find out. Here were things that beggared belief. As well as all the hundreds of labelled boxes Paul kept at home – anything from free toys from cereal boxes to tons of mouldering charity shop kids' clothes – he had stored literally hundreds more here, the contents often inexplicable. One box held nothing other than a single plastic child's chair, another a single electrical extension reel. I also found one containing several garlic presses, explaining why every one I'd ever bought had disappeared.

Another box, ironically, held half a dozen vases, bringing to mind the day when Paul had gone terrifyingly crazy when, having not been able to find a vase in which to put some flowers a friend had bought me, I went and spent a pound on buying a new one. Poignantly, several boxes contained brand new, unused toys, which, as soon as I saw them, I remembered buying. It seemed so weird to see them here, untouched, never played with. Weird but true. When I quizzed the children they confessed that their father would go to them a day or so after whichever birthday, and take the presents from them to put away for 'safe keeping'. None had ever been seen again until now.

The third container was the one that was the real shock, however. It too contained hundreds of stacked cardboard boxes, but the front half had been turned into a kind of office area. When I had a quick look through the papers I realised I was uncovering further evidence of the life Paul had secretly been living; there were papers relating to loans I'd known nothing about - bank accounts ,too - an account at William Hill (he had been betting large sums of money) and a large stack of paper, containing copious notes about how he had planned to disappear. He had planned to get a motorbike (which explained why he'd suddenly decided to take his motorcycle test a few months earlier) then ride to France and go and live with his 'friend' the loan shark. He'd made a note of the fact that he would only keep in touch with his mother, to let her know he was okay, but that was it.

There were other 'solutions', too, all of which made clear of the inevitability of what had happened. 'Suicide' was a constant in all of them.

Most of the three weeks between Paul's death and the funeral passed in a blur; what mostly remains is the feeling I associate with that period – that life had become even more unimaginably complex and terrifying than I'd imagined it could be and that it was too unbearable for him to carry on.

That I had to carry on, however, wasn't negotiable. I was now alone with seven still young, dependent children, all of whom had varying degrees of special needs. They were my only priority and their welfare came above all else, including my own. I couldn't eat anyway. I had a lump in my throat that never seemed to go away and every time I tried to eat anything I physically gagged. My weight at the time of Paul's death was healthy. I was also fit. I would go on to lose two stone by Christmas.

One of the things weighing heaviest upon me was good old-fashioned fear. I was terrified about what might happen at the funeral. Paul's parents had made their feelings very well known. They hated me and held me responsible for Paul's suicide. We had so far not exchanged a single word.

At the time, I was too traumatised by recent events to really take it in; I just remember having this feeling that there was no justice in the world, and accepting that I was powerless to do anything about it. They would think what they thought, and that was their decision, obviously. And I knew what they thought - I was the 'bad guy', as always.

Sanguine though I was about that (at least, in my numbed state) I was still terrified that there could be nastiness at the funeral, both from his parents and possibly from other members of his very large extended family. They were all quite close so there I didn't doubt they were all well aware of how his parents felt about me. I didn't care for myself (I was penniless and desperate, but I had, at least, been liberated) but the thought of anything horrible happening in front of the children was something I couldn't countenance and wouldn't allow.

I expressed my concerns to Vicki, Ingrid and Fiona – all of whom were such incredible stalwarts – and all three agreed that the children needed protecting. After a conflab, they promised me that I had nothing to fear; that all the husbands would create an impenetrable 'armed guard' around us at all times. I also gave strict instructions to the funeral director that Paul's family should be seated at the side of the church, with us in the middle, and my army of friends behind. It was also agreed that the only member of Paul's family to ride in the funeral car with us would be Peter – though this turned out not to be problem anyway, because Paul's parents were apparently unable to bear coming to the house. They had not spoken to me, nor been anywhere near our home since the day Paul had died and, moreover – as I was to learn later – his mother had vowed she never would, as it would remind her of Paul too unbearably. It felt all wrong to me – her grandchildren had to deal with it, didn't they? But at the same time, I wasn't surprised.

The funeral service was to be held in the church where we'd married, which seemed fitting, as it was the only one he really knew. On arrival we waited for the attendants to remove the coffin. As they did one of them slipped and I was terrified they would drop it and in a glimpse of sheer terror I feared Paul's body would fall out in front of the children. They regained their composure and we started the seem-ingly endless walk up the path the doors and then down the aisle I'd walked down 13 years earlier when I vowed to love Paul for better or for worse. The sympathetic faces were unbearable to look at and I tried desperately to hold onto some kind of dignity, as I did my best to support and console the children. Worse was to come as we were taken to our seats. All of Paul's family had been seated behind us, including his parents and all of my friends were seated where they should have been. I glanced over and they all gave me helpless looks that were trying to say sorry. I later discovered that they had all argued as ferociously as they could with the ushers who were adamant that my wishes were to be adhered to and they knew best. I spent the whole service feeling John and Jean's eyes on me, knowing the hatred they were piling in my direction with the hairs on the back of my neck not once laying flat.

The children had all written a poem for Paul, which they were all determined to read out. I had my doubts that when it came to the moment that they would be able to do it, but at the appropriate time they all walked sadly to the front of the church. They took it in turns to say what they had to say. Nikita just couldn't bring herself to utter a word. She struggled to talk to people one-on-one at the best of times but to expect her to talk out loud in front of so many people at such a gruelling time was just impossible for her. To this day she still regrets not being able to read her own words during the service, though I was so incredibly proud of her; she did finally manage to do so at the graveside.

In order to get myself through the day I'd taken a sedative prescribed by the doctor. I knew I had to hold it together as well as I could for the children's sake and knew it would be impossible without help. Everyone struggled through the service and the vicar did her best to say positive things in her sermon but there really isn't much good that can be said about someone taking their own life. My most vivid memory of the whole thing is handing out endless tissues to the children which I'd stuffed into my pockets before we left.

At the end of the service once again the coffin was lifted high onto the shoulders of the pall bearers and carried back out to the waiting hearse. A long procession of cars made their way slowly to the cemetery and everyone gathered around the hole that had been prepared.

A few days before the funeral I took the children to a flower shop in town to choose the wreath for his coffin. They knew they wanted it to say 'daddy' but we had to decide on the flowers from which it would be made. Paul was extremely minimalist so I wanted something to reflect that and asked if they could come up with a wreath made predominantly of laurel leaves intertwined with other greenery with just seven flowers randomly dotted through the wording... one for each child. They all chose a flower to throw into the grave on top of his coffin as well.

Everyone wanted Paul buried not cremated, against my judgement that cremation would be easier for the children in the long term. I acquiesced to everyone's opinion and tried to work out how to make the time at the actual burial a little easier for the children. I came up with an idea which would engage the children giving them something to do which would also feel as though they were doing something nice for Daddy.

I had quite a number of paper punches and bought lots of coloured paper including some metal foil and got them all to punch out thousands of different shapes. They enjoyed the process and we ended up with sizeable bags of 'confetti'. As the coffin was lowered into the ground and they sprinkled the confetti on top, a lot of it missed. The hole in the ground therefore ended up surrounded by pieces of brightly coloured shapes, in stark contrast to the essence of the proceedings. Finally they threw their flowers in, and the ceremony ended.

Peter and I had arranged a wake at the local Cricket Club so we all headed there after leaving the cemetery. All of my friends were already there when our car arrived and I was greeted by Lee and Simon who escorted us all in. I was immediately stopped in my tracks by dozens of people wishing to offer their condolences. I wasn't prepared for this, it hadn't ever crossed my mind that anyone would want to talk to me, I think because I expected everyone who knew Paul would be blaming me along with his parents.

The owner and head teacher from the children's private school were both there and both were so incredibly supportive of us all, kissing and cuddling the children. Various friends who had known Paul for a lot of his life also wanted to talk to me, most of them wanting to know what had happened on the day and why did I think he'd done it. Paul had always portrayed a very different face to the outside world from the one we all knew. To them he was the most wonderful person on the planet, but behind closed doors he was a terrifying, unpredictably violent and controlling figure. We knew the real Paul only too well and it was so hard for us all to hear everyone telling us that the world had lost the most wonderful person. The guilt for the way we all felt was in stark contrast to what people were saying and was almost as overwhelming as the grief and shock.

I eventually managed to sit down at the table that had been commandeered by everyone close to me. The seating area was small so Paul's parents were sitting in a large group of relatives very nearby. I felt so uncomfortable I had a Vodka. (I never drank.) It helped me relax a little though, but Lee saw my keys on top of my handbag and instantly put them in his pocket in case anything happened and I decided to try and drive off. A constant stream of people came over to talk to me, which was so hard, but minute-by-minute I got through the afternoon.

The children were all playing outside on the field, running around laughing and giggling, the relief that the funeral was over very apparent. I watched them playing and wondered what the future held for all of us.

People started drifting away but I wanted to speak to Paul's parents. I wanted to offer them my condolences; after all, they'd lost a son. I didn't know how to approach them but Lee, strong as ever, assured me that I should follow my heart and that if I wanted to speak to them I should.

John wandered outside so I followed him. I walked up to him, put my arms around him and told him how sorry I was. He said he was glad I'd come over as he hadn't known how to do it. We spoke briefly but he seemed anxious that Jean may be angry if he spoke to me for too long. I told him that I loved him and was there for him if he needed me.

Back inside their group was starting to move and Jean stood up. I went over to her, my heart in my mouth and a feeling of panic rising inside me. Before she had a chance to object I'd put my arms around her, told her I loved her and that I was sorry about the loss of her son. She pulled back as forcefully as she could and looked at the ground. Tears fell down her cheeks and she roughly told me that she was far too upset to be able think about anything. Not a 'thank you', not a 'sorry for everything you're all going through as well', nothing. It was only about how *she* felt and it had always been the same.

The children had all spent some time with their Nanna and Grandad during the wake and afterwards they all told me the same thing. That all she spoke about was how she felt and how hurt she was and how she would never get over it.

Another close friend called Sally Jones had also attended the funeral. She was the children's nursery teacher and we had become great friends. Lee drove us all home and made sure we were all safely inside the house before leaving us with Sally. She had arranged with everyone else to stay with us for the evening and make sure we were all ok. Everyone else was exhausted from the past three weeks and needed some space to get their own lives back together and the funeral left everyone feeling totally spent.

The children settled down to watch a DVD to distract themselves, and despite the cold, Sally and I sat outside and talked for hours about Paul and the side to him that she had been so well aware of. She would come sometimes in the holidays and look after the children for a few hours. She'd seen Paul in his own environment and had glimpses of who he really was, partly by the way the children acted around him as well as his own behaviour and the way he spoke to me even in front of her. I felt numb.

The morning after was as uneasy as I knew it would be. The journey back to some kind of normal life would have to begin now - which in some ways felt even harder than it had getting through the past three weeks. An old college friend of Paul's had stayed in town the night before at a hotel and they'd asked if they could come over the next morning to see us. They arrived and I made coffee and Richard asked if we could go for a walk.

We set off across the field and he asked me about Paul. He wanted to know what Paul was like at home as he suspected that all wasn't as it seemed. I tried so hard to explain but it was hard to put into words Pauls' behaviour over the 23 years I'd known him. I gave Richard some examples to try to convey the truth and he then managed to sum Paul up in a few words. 'There was always a conspiracy with Paul' he said. Nothing to Paul had ever been straightforward. If the bank bounced a Direct Debit it was because the bank manager 'had it in for him' for some bizarre reason. If the assistant in a shop was offhand with him, it always because she had something against him. Everyone was secretly jealous of him and no one was to be trusted, and that included his own parents. After years of talking to psychologists and doctors I now know that we were living with a psychopath. We all really did have a lucky escape.

Chapter Twenty-Four
FALLING

The 22nd February 2008 is a day that would be etched in my mind almost as powerfully as the day that Paul had died. It was the day of the inquest. Of course, it didn't change anything, but it had been something I had been dreading, even so. Though it would be a watershed – the official seal on what had happened that day. It would also represent a final truth, and bring everything flooding back.

And it did. Vicki and Fiona accompanied me, their friendship as true as ever. We waited outside in the dingy waiting room, the fustiness hit me and I remember feeling transported back to the day I identified Paul's body. The whole horror of the last few months came flooding back to me and I sat sobbing. Eventually we were called through and the coroner was sitting at a huge table along with several other people I didn't know and also a friend of Paul's called Liz. It was shock to see her there, and I had no idea why she felt the need to go. I still don't know, though I'm sure she had her own reasons.

The coroner opened the inquest and read through the various accounts of the day of Paul's suicide. He then read the statement I'd been asked to make at the time regarding

Paul's mental health and circumstances around the time of his death.

The pathologist who'd done the Post Mortem then outlined their findings and concluded that Paul had died from the loss of blood from the cuts made to his wrist and throat. I was then asked if I had any questions and I said yes.

'Had there been any water in his lungs?' I asked. One question that had been on my mind all along was whether he'd intended to die, and asking this one might just answer it. I wanted to know if he was already dead when he fell into the pond or had he drowned, and when the pathologist confirmed that there was no water evident in his lungs, it was proof to me that Paul's actions had not been a cry for help – he fully intended to end his life, and in such a way that would leave no room for doubt.

The coroner's conclusion was the same as mine. He had intended to kill himself and had gone so far into the woods that he would be hard to find - the cause of his death was therefore recorded as suicide.

There was no comfort in any of this. Just the realisation that he had intended to die and to leave the children that he had wanted so badly. How did a child deal with such a feeling of abandonment? I could only hope that maturity would help them come to terms with the fact that he didn't mean to leave them; it was wholly due to his horribly fractured mind.

We all left and made our way around the corner for a coffee. I sat there in stunned silence, with Vicki and Fiona either side of me, neither knowing what to say either.

Eventually I found the words to thank god it was over, and I was. Only trouble was, it wasn't.

I took a call from Vicki a few days later. 'Have you seen the local paper?' she asked me. 'Only there's a piece on the inquest that I think you need to see.'

I duly went out and bought it and suddenly I knew that the other people at the inquest had been reporters. I opened the paper, nervously hoping that it had been written sensitively for the children's sake, but because of what Vicki had said I was expecting the worst. And that was what I got. They'd gone into great detail about Paul's various injuries and had sensationalised events beyond belief. I felt my heart sink - everyone would read it and it would open all the questions the children dreaded having thrown at them all over again, and at a time when it was all still so raw for them.

I went home upset and stressed, and that quickly turned to anger; so much so that I fired off a letter to the editor. There was nothing to be gained from it – the piece was already out there – but I felt strongly that they should not be allowed to get away with it, not least so that other families involved in such tragedies would not have to have their suffering compounded as ours had.

It achieved nothing, the editor wrote back politely informing me that the inquest had been reported accurately and that was it. So I decided to take the matter to the Press Complaints Commission. It was a small victory when they found for me, but a precious one. It resulted in a visible apology but, most important, to an undertaking to cover similar stories in future with much more tact and sensitivity.

Little by little I was inching back to some kind of normality and it was little things such as fighting my corner with the local paper that provided regular shots in the arm; all about gathering strength, and feeling useful.

That March, my friend Fiona had to have an MRI scan for an ongoing problem with her back. She'd had one before and was so terrified she wasn't sure she'd be able to go through with it so, having had MRI scans myself and knowing full well why she was frightened, I offered to go with her and support her through it. She'd been given a mild sedative, which did help a lot, but as I sat close to her through the 40 minutes of it, distracting her and stroking her head, it occurred to me that I was perhaps getting more from it than she was, such was my joy at being able to give something back to a friend who'd cared for me so tirelessly for so long.

But my 'recovery' from the trauma of Paul's suicide was fragile. The endless rounds of meetings and assessments for Nikita continued unabated and little things like ordering Osborn's special night pants (he was still wetting the bed and needed protection at night, as a lot of autistic children do) were becoming chores that I increasingly felt I just couldn't cope with.

Simple phone calls such as those were increasingly feeling beyond me; it felt difficult enough even to pick up the phone, let alone talk to another person at the other end of it. The feeling was getting worse and worse and everything was slipping behind, because anything I could avoid doing I would. Was I turning into Paul? Burying my head in the sand? I was certainly putting off dealing with problem, which just created more problems, and very soon it was spiralling out of control.

The doctor had changed the antidepressants he'd put me on, but nothing seemed to be changing in terms of how I felt. I wasn't improving and I knew I desperately needed to. We were going to a Haven caravan park in Doniford, Somerset in the Easter holiday and I hoped that the break would give me a much-needed lift. We were still making our treks to Assist in Rugby and this was taking it out of me as well. I'd had another comprehensive round of blood tests done to see if there was anything physically wrong with me but as always they came back clear.

The holiday itself was relatively uneventful. We went on day trips, went swimming, just chilled in and around our chalet, and it seemed as though the children were all enjoying it, which I remember thinking was good, but I was like a cat on hot bricks. I just couldn't relax at all and permanently had that gut-wrenching, hollowed out feeling: as though I'd just been told someone had died. It never went away and with it came a sensation I can only describe feeling as though worms were burrowing their way through my brain. It was horrific and sleeping was almost impossible. I felt exhausted along with everything else and even the simple task of cooking a meal felt like an insurmountable mountain. I had no idea how I was going to go on feeling like this without something giving.

And I was right. Of course something was going to give. We returned home, and to the business of the rest of our lives. And finally something did give. It was me.

I don't know why I still feel a sense of shock at what happened, because, on the outside, looking in, it seemed inevitable. It was as if I had been trapped permanently in one long bleak midwinter. With seven children and their multiple needs to get my head around, I needed to be alert and on the case, but it was as if I was dragging myself through treacle. But still I'd doggedly carried on; college applications, dental appointments, statementing for Nikita, even flu jabs – that was my job; to find solutions, just as it had been when Paul was still alive, and I'd had to fire-fight in so many ways.

One particular trigger for overwhelming anxiety was the sound of helicopters. I only had to hear one to feel weak with anxiety – I would feel faint, cry uncontrollably and go stiff with terror. And though I'd never before noticed, it seemed we were on some sort of helicopter flight path, so these feelings would ambush me several times a day.

My breakdown, when it came, was probably long overdue. And probably had to happen for us to move on. It happened at the end of April, rather unexpectedly, when I was visiting a potential new special school for Nikita with a lovely lady from the NHS autism team.

I knew Nikita wouldn't cope in a mainstream secondary school, so getting her into one that could support her properly was one of my most important priorities, and Round Oak School in Warwick seemed the perfect place. It was very small, with only around ten children in each class, and as soon as we arrived I had this strong sense of community; a feeling that here was a place where she would feel safe and supported. They had fabulous facilities but more important was the calibre of the staff. Right away

I got this sense that they would be able to deal with her complex needs and help her reach her potential; that they both listened and understood. I also saw several children during our tour who put me in mind of Nikita, confirming the gut feeling I had that this was exactly the sort of place where she would thrive.

Was that the trigger? The sense that I *had* to get that place for her come what may? I don't know, but what I do know was that by the time we'd finished the tour, I must have been looking strange, acting oddly, or a combination of both because while the lady from the Autism team and I were walking out into the car park, chatting – as far as I could tell – about how nice the school was, about Paul, about things generally at home, she began looking at me strangely.

'Are you okay?' she asked me, a look of concern on her face.

'Yes, I'm fine,' I replied automatically. It was, after all, my stock answer to any question about my wellbeing.

'Are you sure?' she persisted. 'You seem terribly upset. You're crying, Vikie,' she added gently. 'You've been crying all this time.'

She then asked my permission to ring my Social Worker and ask her to pop round. And I agreed that she could, albeit reluctantly. Perhaps she was right, I thought. Perhaps I *could* do with some help, though I had no idea what form that might take.

I said farewell to her and went back to town on autopilot, picking up the six children who needed collecting from their various schools, and then driving home. Once there, as they scattered to their rooms to get out of their uniforms, I walked into the kitchen.

I remember waking across to the hob by the sink, and standing next to it, rooted to the spot. It was the strangest thing; I was fully conscious, but I simply couldn't step away from it. I felt paralysed, powerless to move. I had no idea what was wrong with me, or what to do about it, only vaguely aware of a knock at the door and one of the children going to answer it and then two women (one I recognised as my social worker) coming in and asking me who my doctor was. She was calling them before I had any idea what was going on and, taking me by the arm, led me out to her car, while the other social worker stayed with the children. We must have driven into town then but I have no recollection of it; only a vague memory of a conversation about antidepressants and Prozac and how I must be taken off it straight away.

When we arrived home - again, I have no clear memory of the journey - she put me straight to bed, telling me that the doctor would visit tomorrow, and I was happy to stay there because I didn't feel able to do anything; I felt as ill as I'd felt in a long time. I remember lying there vaguely pondering if I had flu or some kind of virus but nothing seemed to add up; my brain felt as if it was hardly functioning.

My phone rang about 9pm and I struggled to answer it. It was my friend Mandy, whose fitness class I always go to on a Wednesday evening. And when I hadn't turned up, she knew something must be up – if I was unable to make a class, I'd always let her know in advance. She asked me what was wrong. 'I honestly don't know,' I remember telling her. And within a few minutes of the call ending she was right there in my bedroom; yet another person took one look at me and immediately looked panicky. All most odd, I remember thinking, largely bemused.

My friend Mandy took charge of things, completely. She came to the house first thing the following morning to get to get the children all to school and had them fill her in on what the social worker had said. They told her as best they could and she told me what she had planned with them. I meanwhile, lay upstairs, oblivious. I felt drugged, as though someone had given me something that was rendering me unable to think coherently or move my body the way I was telling it to. I couldn't stop crying, either – and I wasn't a crier. I never had been. But now if felt like I'd never be able to stop.

I was kind of aware of various children coming and going, but I was in such a daze I really have no idea what was going on, till sometime that morning, when Mandy ushered a lady into my room. She sat at the end of my bed and talked to me about how I was feeling. I was in a total stupor and could barely make sense of what she wanted from me so Mandy was answering a lot of the questions, and at the end of what felt like an exhausting eternity she announced that she would call the ambulance.

What ambulance? Now my brain seemed to snap to attention. Why did I need an ambulance? Where were they taking me? I asked her what the hell was going on and she told me I'd had a breakdown. I was mentally, emotionally and physically exhausted and, because I refused to stop, my brain and body had forced me to.

She went off to ring the hospital to arrange for me to be admitted and I hysterically I begged Mandy to stop her. How could I possibly go into hospital and leave the children? They would be taken into care and they'd been through enough. That would be the last straw in their young lives, and it couldn't happen. And it wouldn't happen. Not over my dead body.

It didn't happen. My fears were heeded and we were spared. A way was found, to my great relief, for me to be treated at home, supported by a team to whom I owe so very much. Social Services were brilliant. Far from making me feel that they might imminently take my children from me, they were incredibly quick to step in and support us as a family, and did so much for us, both practically and financially. Emotionally, it was a period that marked a watershed for all of us. Always so independent, I'd long baulked at the idea of needing anybody for support, but with support came the freedom to get myself back together, and the strength to properly fight for what my family needed, and I couldn't have been more grateful. I made a mental note that I would find some way of repaying it.

Most important, in the short term, was proper counselling. Unsurprisingly, we all had post-traumatic stress disorders to some degree, and help with this made a big difference to all of us. All of us went for trauma counselling, and little by little we saw the benefits. We were also incredibly lucky in having such marvellous friends, including Carl, who had worked for the business since 1998 and who was a tower of strength in keeping it going; talking to clients, arranging bookings, delivering equipment and running events. He even moved into the Atlas for a time so he could be on hand to organise everything, which meant Big Indoor Games survived when I really thought it wouldn't, and gave me precious time and space in which to concentrate on the children and their needs.

That the children were my priority had never been in question, but that was now truer than perhaps it had ever been. And, in the short term, there was one hurdle that I was determined I was going leap. To get Nikita that precious place at Round Oak School. And I knew I had a challenge on my hands.

It would be the first of many challenges I would be tackling over the coming years, but I was feeling stronger day by day now. I knew I had to be.

Chapter Twenty-Five

'THE BEST DAY EVER'

It was the summer of 2008 before I properly began to feel well again, and as soon as I did, I was determined we would have a family holiday that wasn't marred for the children by my being so unwell. Holidays were precious but had been few over the years, mainly the odd trip to Butlins or Haven (usually minus Paul) using the Tesco Clubcard vouchers I'd managed to amass.

I booked another Haven caravan for a week, back in Doniford in Somerset, and I don't think it was till I saw how excited the kids were that it hit me just how bad things had been for them. I'd been ill for so long, and it had taken its toll. And my recovery didn't just mean I was better and more present for them. It also marked the end a period of terrible fear for all of them. While we were living through it, I probably hadn't fully grasped just how close we'd come to them all having to go into care; perhaps I hadn't allowed myself to.

For them, I now realised, that possibility had all been too real. And as I recovered, I would still wake in the small hours, bathed in sweat, when it began sinking in just how close I might have come to losing them. And them me. And they had already lost so much.

The previous summer, the one preceding Paul's suicide, had been so different. I had taken the children to the Haven caravan site that August too, determined to get them away for at least a few days. That they needed respite and sunshine was the thought uppermost in my mind, as Paul and I continued the laborious process of dismantling our lives together - a process that had begun with that sudden revelation outside a pound shop and which was going to end – or so I'd thought – by the end of that year, when the sale of the house was finally completed and we went our separate ways.

It hadn't been the happiest of weeks, despite the clemency of the West Country weather on that occasion, as the days were punctuated at regular intervals by telephone calls between Paul and I, discussing the potential sale of the house, how much buyers were offering, and what was going to happen to such money as would be scraped together as a result. And as all this needed to be done without the children knowing what was happening (Paul was adamant we told them nothing till a sale was agreed) it led to frequent unexplained absences every time my mobile rang - hardly conducive to a sense of security.

In the end it had been Paul who had filed for divorce that summer, even though I'd told him more than once I wasn't asking for that. In the first instance, I just wanted us to physically separate; he was hardly 'living' with us in the sense that most people would use the term in any case, and when he did go through a period of wanting to interact with the children, it was always so fraught with tension that it could never be good for them – they had become much too frightened of him by now.

My short-term goal was therefore to simply remove them from the unpredictability and corrosiveness of their home environment. And, having found a buyer shortly after our return, Paul was finally ready to tell them what was going on; that they were going to have to say goodbye to the house.

By now his behaviour had become even more bizarre and volatile, to the point where we were now tiptoeing round him literally as well as metaphorically, and one of my sharpest and most upsetting memories of that period was of Osborn, his only son, and a child who really needed a father's input, going over to stand next to him while he was working one day, holding a book and obviously wishing to ask him something. Paul completely ignored him, even though he was standing right next to him, and continued to do so for ten long minutes. Too scared to intervene, for fear of making things worse for Osborn, I could only stand and will his father to communicate. Even a 'go away, I'm busy' would have been infinitely preferable to this chilling display of Paul sitting there consciously pretending his son wasn't there. Even worse, though, was that Osborn had been so conditioned to total submissiveness that he didn't even have the confidence to speak. Not even to quietly ask 'dad?'.

That excruciating ten minutes, after which Osborn quietly walked away and into my arms for a cuddle, only added to my resolve that we must get away, *fast*.

But before that, it was necessary to explain to all the children what had happened, what was happening now and what would happen next. I wanted us to sit them down and tell them together; it seemed the only logical way to proceed.

But Paul was having none of it. Though he agreed we should tell them together, he didn't want *them* to be together, his strange logic being that they should be told individually, one by one. To this end, he made then all sit in the sitting room, while we sat in the garden, and called them out, starting with Jamie, and working his way down by age.

It was a particularly upsetting piece of cruelty, whether it was his intention or not, and I couldn't help but think that it was much more about him than about them. Their distress – they were forbidden from telling those that were yet to come in what had happened – seemed to take second place to his need to conduct his 'meetings' with self-indulgent military precision. He was also keen to make it clear that leaving the house wasn't what he wanted but that our financial position was so dire that there was no choice. Needless to say, the children were deeply distraught – particularly about leaving the only home they'd ever known - but such was their fear of him by now that none dared disobey him. The same, sadly, applied to me as well.

The whole process took something like an hour. By now, I didn't know what to think. Such peculiar behaviour left me upset but also completely bewildered; as if he'd finally lost what little grasp on emotional reasoning he'd ever had. He'd always been an intermittent presence in the children's' lives - interacting with them and then dismissing them for weeks at a time - but by now their relationships were disintegrating fast. I remember thinking then that, in his head, he'd probably already left them. Though, as we were to find out less than a month later, his coming departure would be more complete than that.

It felt so good to be back in Somerset, because it was a place that held lots of happy memories for the children, which they badly needed in order to counteract the bad. Even happy memories of Paul, who, a couple of times, had driven down to join us on holiday there. And I was glad of that. Even if he had only ever stayed a day or two, he was at least part of their small store of things to look back on where their father was concerned and be able to smile.

The weather wasn't perfect – more dull and drizzly than wall-to-wall sunshine. But as that had never been a deterrent to us doing anything, on the third day, which was a Sunday, we donned cagoules and headed down to the beach, with the idea of beachcombing as we ambled down to Watchet. I'd been told that it was no more than a 20-minute walk, which I reasoned would be just right for Osborn and Pippa. Which was to turn out to be somewhat optimistic.

Doniford beach is a brilliant place for fossils. We'd taken a couple of plastic carrier bags and they were soon filled to bursting – mostly with small fossils, pretty shells and bits of driftwood but also with Osborn's favourite – rocks. They had such fun digging treasures from the retaining wall (possibly illegal!) using whatever implements they had to hand, and when they weren't doing that they were rescuing stranded mussels that had been washed up on the beach, attached to clumps of seaweed. What the mussels thought about this is anyone's guess, but I couldn't have been happier watching all seven children dashing back and forth reuniting them with the water.

Doing anything with seven kids in tow is always going to be something of a military exercise, but I think it was perhaps that day above every one that came before or have happened since that I realised that not only had I recovered from my breakdown but that, actually, I was doing okay - that I could mother them on my own. I could take care of them and meet their complex needs, if not exactly with my eyes shut, at least with confidence and relative ease. It was the best feeling I'd had in a very long time.

'How on earth are we going to get across here, mum?' Kacie wanted to know, when halfway along the beach we were faced with a fast flowing watercourse that was running from the retaining wall down to the sea. It wasn't that large but it was fairly deep and, given the vagaries of the weather, I didn't like the idea of any of them slipping and getting drenched.

'Easy!' said Lorie promptly proving her point by leaping the six metre wide expanse in half a dozen coltish bounds, and without getting her trainers too wet. Jamie promptly followed, as did Kacie and Mirie.

'Yes, easy for you,' I pointed out. 'But what about the others? That deep bit in the middle's far too wide for them to jump.'

'Yes, what about us?' Nikita said. 'I can't jump anywhere near that far! And what about Osborn and Pippa?'

Nikita was right. It might be easy for the older ones, but it was no small matter for the little ones, especially Osborn and Pippa, because of their CP. Cue a long family discussion about the safety of wading through deep, fast flowing water generally, and further discussion about whether we should give up and head back. But no one wanted to turn back. They were having too much fun. And with the prospect of an ice-cream once we got to Watchet in prospect, talk soon turned to strategy, and how best we could achieve it.

And achieve it we did, palaver though it was, what with socks and trainers having to be removed, trouser legs rolled up, and further debate about possibly jettisoning some of the heavier, rockier 'treasure', before piggybacks were agreed.

This was particularly hard on poor Osborn, whose haul of treasure was deemed much too heavy.

'But it we leave it here, someone might steal it!' he complained.

(In fact, he even went back the following day to look, but without success.)

But needs must, and after half an hour we were all on the right side of the river and, bar the small pang of regret about the rocks on Osborn's part, our spirits could not have been higher. Which was just as well, as they were about to be tested further still.

We duly made it to the Watchet end of the beach, where we were rewarded with the best fossil of all; around six feet in length, it was embedded deeply into the rock, and had obviously been some sort of primeval sea-creature. It was astonishingly well-preserved, and we spent ages standing marveling at it and even – mad, looking back - wondering if the local people knew it was there. So engrossed were we, in fact, that it had completely escaped our notice that the incoming tide was about to cut us off from the quay steps.

Cue another major challenge as we scrambled back over the huge, slippery rocks, trying to carry Osborn and Pippa between us. And if we thought the rocks were treacherous, they were as nothing to the steep steps up to the quay, which were equally slimy and slippery, and helpfully, came minus any kind of handrail. Or indeed, health and safety warning; ascend here and take your life into your hands!

Thankfully, we made it, but now we had a new problem. We were in Watchet when we needed to be in Doniford, and the beach we'd walked along to get here was almost completely submerged. I chastised myself now: why had I never considered this? Not being local I'd never even thought about tides, and we were now going to have to pay for my ignorance. There was no way of heading back yet.

'Don't worry,' I told the children, while mentally counting the cash I'd slung into my cagoule pocket just before we'd left. 'We'll forget the ice-cream and go and get something proper to eat instead, shall we? I'm sure there'll be a café somewhere nearby.'

There was a collective groan, but I knew it would make more sense to eat something hot and nutritious. It was already half past two and they were all cold and wet. So much for our 40-minute, maximum-an-hour, stroll. We'd already been out since before noon!

But within just a few steps we were into the village proper and the children were immediately cheered at the sight of a little café up ahead.

It was a typically seaside-y sort of place, very small, rather tired-looking; the sort of place you can find in seaside towns everywhere, and which looked liked it hadn't changed in 30 years. And once they'd got over the shock of their eight new arrivals rearranging all the tables, they set to work happily enough, bringing us eight lots of beans on toast. And as we waited, we were, as ever, the centre of attention, with other diners all wanting to know where we'd come from, how we'd got there and – as ever – whether all seven children really were my own.

Our late lunch, naturally, went down a storm. And now we were refreshed, all that was left, then, was to see what the tide was up to. Perhaps by now it would have gone out sufficiently that we could go back along the beach. Looking back, I don't know what I must have been thinking, given that the slimy steps to the quay had already given me an obvious clue, but I was stupid enough to parade them all back down the road to the sea wall, where, the tide was of course, even higher than it had been.

Which left us stuck. It was a case of either hanging around for hours, or finding some other way of getting home. Not that there was any question of walking it via the road. It was a good couple of miles, I knew, mostly via a busy A roads without a pavement, and even had it been safe, the little ones were way too tired.

There was nothing for it. There were no buses that I knew of – this was a Sunday, in a sleepy corner of Somerset. So we would have to get a cab.

We trooped back to the café to enquire, and handily there was a card from a local taxi firm pinned up on the café wall. So while the children used the loo, I phoned the number on my mobile. And if it had to be two trips, so be it, I decided. I had cash at the caravan. I could simply nip inside to get money to pay the drivers when we arrived.

'Fine,' he said, after confirming that, happily, he had an eight seater. 'I can probably be there by 7.30pm.'

'7.30pm?' I asked incredulously. 'But that's still four hours away!'

'Sorry, love,' he said. 'That's the first time I can fit you in. I've already got bookings, you see.'

I felt my face fall. 'Is there another taxi firm I can call, perhaps?'

'Sorry, love,' he said again. 'I'm the only taxi round here. People tend to book me a few days in advance,' he added helpfully.

Which was no help at all, of course. But then a solution occurred to me - there was a steam railway, wasn't there? And I was pretty sure it stopped in Doniford. If we were lucky, that might just be the answer. I duly rounded up the kids and we headed towards the station, pleased that this extra bit of adventure had boosted their energy, and keeping quiet about the new worry that had now risen to the surface - that our luck might have run out, and the last train of the day might have already gone; it was only really a tourist attraction, after all.

Thankfully, after half an hour, a train did turn up, and I managed to scrabble together just enough cash to pay the guard. When the train dropped us, however, it was to find that Doniford 'station' wasn't a station at all. It was just a 'halt' in a field, which was connected to the main road by a long muddy lane. Having no choice, we took it, but we were then faced with a dilemma. We were now on a main road but had no idea which way to walk. By now we were having to carry both Pippa and Osborn, the older girls taking turns with me to do so.

It was a scary walk. The road was narrow and winding, with several terrifying blind bends, and I was herding seven children, two in arms and somewhat heavy. So every time a car sped by my heart was in my mouth. Worse still, as we trudged on, was that I had no way of knowing whether we were even going in the right direction. Would we still be out trudging the lanes when it was dark?

I'd just decided it might be best if I tried to find a safe place for them to shelter while I walked ahead to fetch the car, when they all squealed in unison. 'There it is, mum! There it is!

And sure enough it was – we could just make out the Haven flag fluttering in the distance. At this point I asked the children if they wanted to wait for me to bring the car back but, buoyed by this news, they were all determined to see it through. They were such troupers! We finally arrived back in the caravan half an hour later, and collapsed in a big heap, completely shattered. But despite the promised ice-cream having failed to materialise, there was still so much excited chatter about the various traumas and debacles - in that way that children do when they triumph over adversity.

'That was one of the best days of my life, ever!' announced Osborn.

'Mine as well!' everyone clamoured to agree.

And they kept on repeating it as the evening wore on; that it had been one of the best days they'd had, *ever*. It made me feel so happy I thought I might burst.

'We couldn't have done *anything* like this,' Lorie said, 'not if Dad had been around.'

Which allowed a wisp of sadness to creep in, which was understandable and right, as they all quietly thought about what they'd lost. But it then sparked a new conversation, of a very different kind, as they soberly sat and contemplated, in that forensic way children do, how many fun things we'd done as a family since their father had died.

So, on balance, it had been a very happy day, we all agreed; we'd had the most fun we'd had in *such* a long time, even in the midst of our tide-based adversity. But as I sat among my beloved children (the family of my own; the family that I never thought I'd have) I realised that at the same time, it was very, very sad that so much of their childhood so far had been so horribly blighted.

So far, at least. It wasn't going to be that way any longer. I was strong again now, and I knew my children were strong as well. Sad though it was to say – and it felt terribly sad to say it – but we all felt so much happier and more empowered. Now it was *our* time. Now it was *their* time.

And, from now on, things would be better.

EPILOGUE

If that day out in Doniford proved to be a turning point for all of us - which it did - we certainly didn't turn around to see a vista made of rolling meadows, pretty sunsets and happy-ever-afters. Though it would mark the point at which I finally took control of my own destiny, it was also the start of an uncertain and scary future. I was truly alone now - my only remaining family, bar my children, comprising an elderly uncle in Manchester and my severely autistic brother Tony (who was now barely speaking to me anyway, since finding out how Paul had duped him over the loan).

In the short term, things felt as if they were starting to get better; we found out, on that same holiday, that Nikita had had her place confirmed at Round Oak, and though it would be three months before she looked at, let alone interacted with another person there, once she settled, she began to flourish and find her way. The other children, too, began to grow in confidence, once their various needs were being met. It was a lot of work, but we finally got statements for Osborn in 2009 and Pippa in 2010, meaning they could both attend a superb special school called Exhall Grange. Lorie and Mirie, ever the drama queens, also found their métier. In 2011 they both started Drama School.

But there was never any question that some of the biggest challenges in our lives were still to come. In the five years since Paul's death, life has been a very different sort of rollercoaster, and the process of self-discovery is still ongoing. It's a work-in-progress for me every bit as much as for my children, involving some hard times, of course, but also a great deal of laughter. In fact, it's true to say that we've also had some incredibly comical moments - something which I guess, as for most families, is inevitable.

Yes, it's been an up and down, and undoubtedly emotionally demanding few years, but there's been a solid core of responsibility that's given me an enormous sense of purpose. My main focus was always be the best mother I could to my seven children, an ambition that only intensified once I was their sole parent. And, with so many of them to care for (Jamie has only just turned 23 now, and still lives with us) I never thought I was going to have a quiet and uneventful life. And fate saw to it that my expectations were met.

Incredibly – and I wonder; might this be a record? - six of my children suffered appendicitis over the years, and had surgery in the space of four – two of them only a week apart. Not that they weren't used to medical attention: with them all requiring support for their myriad different needs, my weekdays were always dominated by visits to hospitals and schools, and still are. An average week can still see me attending perhaps nine or ten different meetings – in a single week last year, I counted 17!

Not that I'm after anyone's sympathy. Empathy would be wonderful – there must be many women who've faced challenges like mine, I'm sure! But ultimately, I'm well aware that my circumstances are self-inflicted, and that it's up to me to help my kids achieve the best and most productive lives they can. My greatest hope is that, by reading my story, others will be able to reflect on their own lives and choices and perhaps feel enabled as a result. If this book does one thing, I want that one thing to be that it inspires.

I also hope it's made for a truthful, engaging read, even if it has, up to now, been a life less ordinary. In some lives, I've come to realise that you really *couldn't* make it up. And what do you know? With all these children and the adventures we've had along the way, it's still been holding true ever since.

But that's another story.

ABOUT THE AUTHORS

Vikie Shanks

I was born in 1958 in Aden (now the South Yemen) as my father was stationed with the RAF there at the time. I was the youngest of three children, having two older brothers; Philip, who was 13 years older than me, and Tony who was two years older and autistic.

We moved around, as all forces families do, until we settled in a little village called Waterbeach near Cambridge when my father was posted there when I was five.

At the age of 17 I moved to London to start work in Harrods as a trainee buyer but left after a year and started work as a croupier. After two years working in London and a further year in Spain I became a full time model.

When I was 25 I met Paul, who was to become my husband and father to my seven children. We moved from London to the Midlands in 1986. It transpired over the years that he was mentally very unstable. He committed suicide at the age of 51. I have been a single mother to the children ever since, continuing to run the corporate entertainment business that Paul and I ran together when he was alive.

To find out about my Autism One on One support group and to read my blog about life in the 'Mad Shanks Household' please visit www.vikieshanks.com

Lynne Barrett-Lee (Ghostwriter)

Previously a successful novelist, Lynne Barrett-Lee has been a full time ghostwriter for the past seven years, and has co-authored 14 Sunday Times bestsellers. She has also penned two writing guides, both published by Thistle, based on the creative writing courses she teaches in Cardiff. Lynne also writes a weekly column for the Western Mail Weekend magazine.

To find out more about Lynne's ghostwriting projects please visit www.lynnebarrett-lee.com

Made in the USA
Middletown, DE
26 October 2017